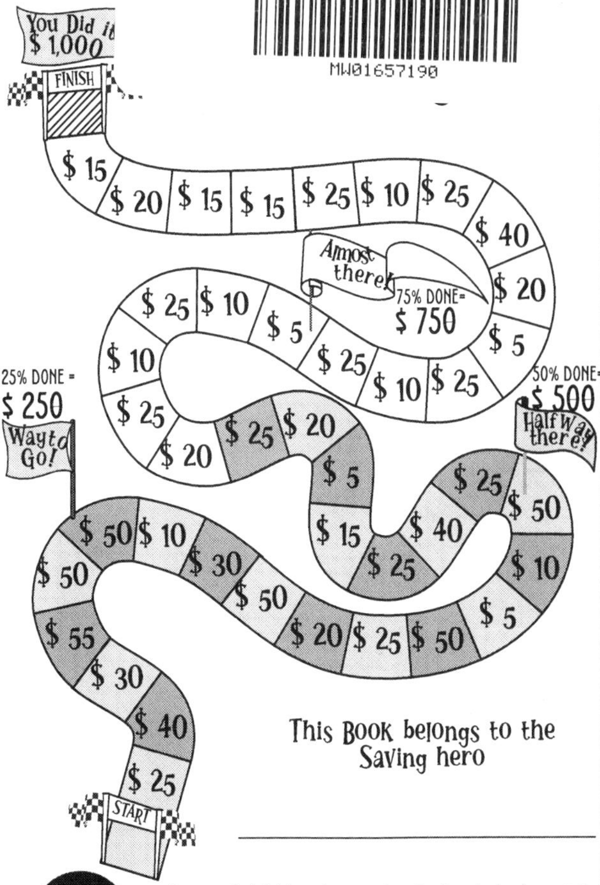

This Book belongs to the Saving hero

Aurora Publishing is passionate in designing and creating Logbooks, Record books, Journals with unique and effective designs to bring you that extra awesomeness you always wished for

Saving money made easier and enjoyable with this awesome savings challenge bundle that will help keep you motivated on your saving journey. Use this collection of Money Saving Challenge trackers to help you save for those unexpected expenses and make the savings a habit in life.

Depending on the challenge, choose any amount and save it for a particular week or day. Once you have that amount saved, simply color in the icon on each savings challenge and see your progress!
Start your savings journey!

This awesome challenges bundle will help to Keep track of the progress as you crush your money-saving goals!

There are various interesting Challenges designed to make your saving journey fun and enjoyable. You can navigate the challenges through their time duration, total Saving amount or per saving amount. Following are the awesome saving challenges included.

30 Days Money Saving Challenges

- $100 Saving Challenge - 2 Challenges
- $500 Saving Challenge - 2 Challenges
- $1000 Saving Challenge -2 Challenges
- No Spend Month Challenge -2 Challenges
- Set your own challenge -4 Challenges

50 Days Money Saving Challenges

- $1 Savings Challenge (Save $50) - 2 Challenges
- $2 Savings Challenge (Save $100) - 2 Challenges
- $3 Savings Challenge (Save $150) - 2 Challenges
- $4 Savings Challenge (Save $200) - 2 Challenges
- $5 Savings Challenge (Save $250) - 2 Challenges
- $10 Savings Challenge (Save $500) - 2 Challenges
- $15 Savings Challenge (Save $750) - 2 Challenges
- $20 Savings Challenge (Save $1,000) - 2 Challenges
- $25 Savings Challenge (Save $1,250) - 2 Challenges
- $30 Savings Challenge (Save $1,500) - 2 Challenges
- $40 Savings Challenge (Save $2,000) - 2 Challenges
- $50 Savings Challenge (Save $2,500) - 2 Challenges
- Set your own challenge - 4 Challenges

100 Days Money Saving Challenges

- $500 Saving Challenge - 2 Challenges
- $1000 Saving Challenge - 2 Challenges
- $5000 Savings Challenge - 2 Challenges
- Set your own challenge - 4 Challenges

26 Weeks Money Saving Challenges

- +$ 1 Forward Saving Challenge (Save $351) - 2 Challenges
- -$ 1 Backward Saving Challenge (Save $351) - 2 Challenges
- +$ 2 Forward Savings Challenge (Save $702) - 2 Challenges
- -$ 2 Backward Savings Challenge (Save $702) - 2 Challenges
- $2000 Saving Challenge - 2 Challenges
- $2500 Savings Challenge - 2 Challenges
- $3000 Savings Challenge - 2 Challenges
- $5000 Savings Challenge - 2 Challenges
- $10000 Savings Challenge - 2 Challenges
- $15000 Savings Challenge - 2 Challenges
- Set your own challenge - 4 Challenges

52 Weeks Money Saving Challenges

- +$ 1 Forward Saving Challenge (Save $ 1,378) - 2 Challenges
- -$ 1 Backward Saving Challenge (Save $ 1,378) - 2 Challenges
- +$ 2 Forward Savings Challenge (Save $2756) - 2 Challenges
- -$ 2 Backward Savings Challenge (Save $2756) - 2 Challenges
- $2000 Saving Challenge - 2 Challenges
- $2500 Savings Challenge - 2 Challenges
- $3000 Savings Challenge - 2 Challenges
- $5000 Savings Challenge - 2 Challenges
- $6000 Savings Challenge - 2 Challenges
- $10000 Savings Challenge - 2 Challenges
- $15000 Savings Challenge - 2 Challenges
- $20000 Savings Challenge - 2 Challenges
- Set your own challenge - 2 Challenges

Aurora Publishing is passionate in designing and creating Logbooks, Record books, Journals with unique and effective designs to bring you that extra awesomeness you always wished for

30 Day Money Saving Challenges

- $100 Saving Challenge - 2 Challenges
- $500 Saving Challenge - 2 Challenges
- $1000 Saving Challenge -2 Challenges
- No Spend Month Challenge -2 Challenges*
- Set your own challenge -4 Challenges*

*** No Spend Month Challenge**
A period of time when you commit to not spending money on non-essentials

*** Set your own challenge**
During this challenge you can save any amount or commit to any saving related activity. Depending on the challenge you decide to go forward, simply color in the icons accordingly.

Each challenge has a starting point and a finishing point. However, only in some challenges, you need to follow a specific path, and in others you can choose your own path to reach the finishing point. Once you start a challenge, keep going, do not break, and always try to finish within the given time period.
Per day/week saving amount is the same for some challenges and it is different for other challenges. So, depending on the challenge, choose the amount and save it for a particular week or day. Once you have that amount saved, simply color in the icon on each savings challenge and see your progress!

Happy Saving Journey !

30-Day Savings Challenges

Duration = 30 Days Goal = $ 100

Start date - . . . . Finish date - . . . .

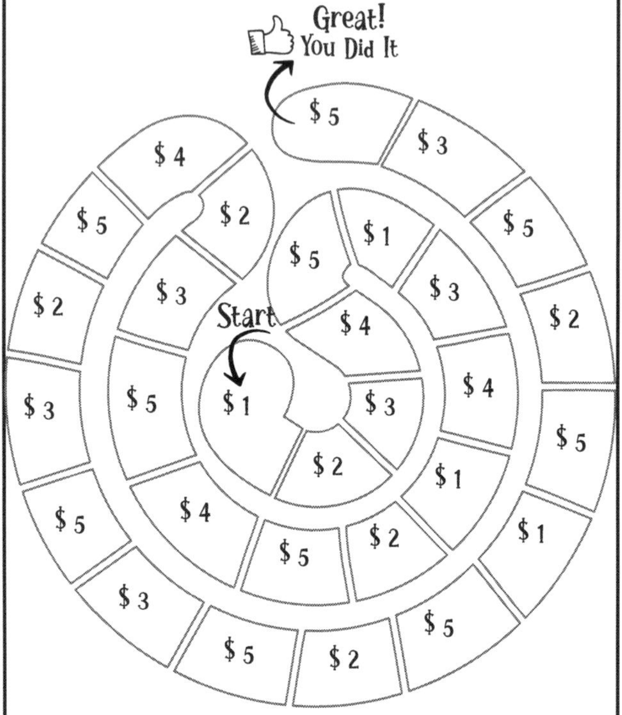

Duration = 30 Days Goal = $ 100

Start date - . . . . Finish date - . . . .

Reach for the Stars

Duration = 30 Days Goal = $ 500

Start date - .... Finish date - ....

Super!
You made it

$ 20 $ 30 $ 15 $ 5

$ 15 $ 5 $ 25 $ 10

$ 25 $ 10

My Saving

$ 20 $ 5

$ 15 $ 5 $ 25

$ 25 $ 30 $ 20 $ 30

$ 5

Journey!

$ 25 $ 15

Let's start
the journey
here!

$ 10 $ 20 $ 5 $ 10

$ 5 $ 15 $ 25 $ 30

Duration = 30 Days Goal = $ 500

Start date - . . . . Finish date - . . . .

Awesome! You Did It

$ 10 $ 25

$ 20 $ 5 $ 30 $ 5

$ 5 $ 25 $ 25 $ 20

$ 25 $ 15 $ 20 $ 5

$ 5 $ 10 $ 30

$ 30 $ 5 $ 30 $ 5 $ 25

$ 30 $ 10

$ 10 $ 20 $ 15 $ 25

Start $ 5 $ 10

Duration = 30 Days　　Goal = $ 1000

Start date - . . . .　　Finish date - . . . .

Great! You made it

$ 50	$ 20	$ 40	$ 35	$ 55	$ 25
$ 25	$ 35	$ 30	$ 20	$ 40	$ 55
$ 55	$ 15	$ 50	$ 5	$ 45	$ 30
$ 30	$ 45	$ 40	$ 35	$ 55	$ 40
$ 5	$ 10	$ 20	$ 30	$ 25	$ 35

let's begin here

Duration = 30 Days

Goal = $ 1000

Start date - . . . .

Finish date - . . . .

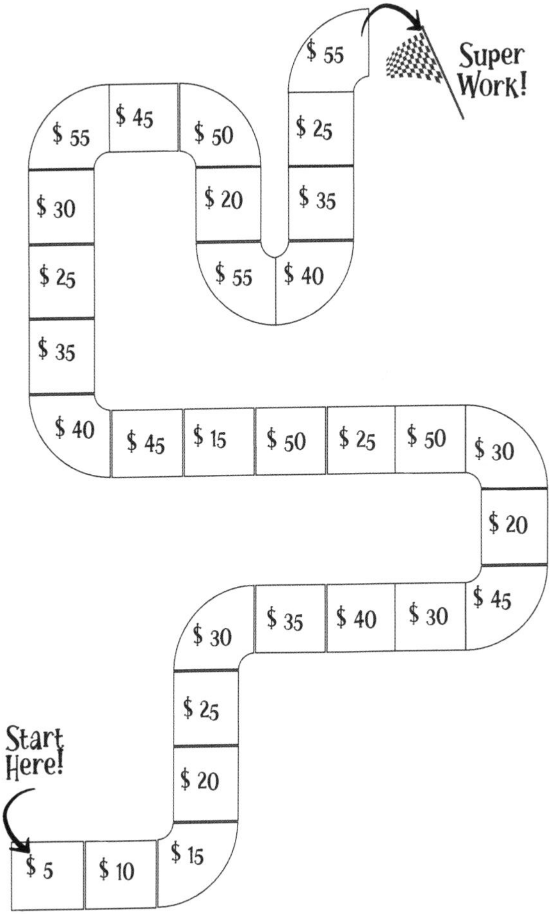

Duration = 30 Days | Goal = NO SPEND

Start date - .... | Finish date - ....

Duration = 30 Days

Goal = NO SPEND

Start date - . . . .

Finish date - . . . .

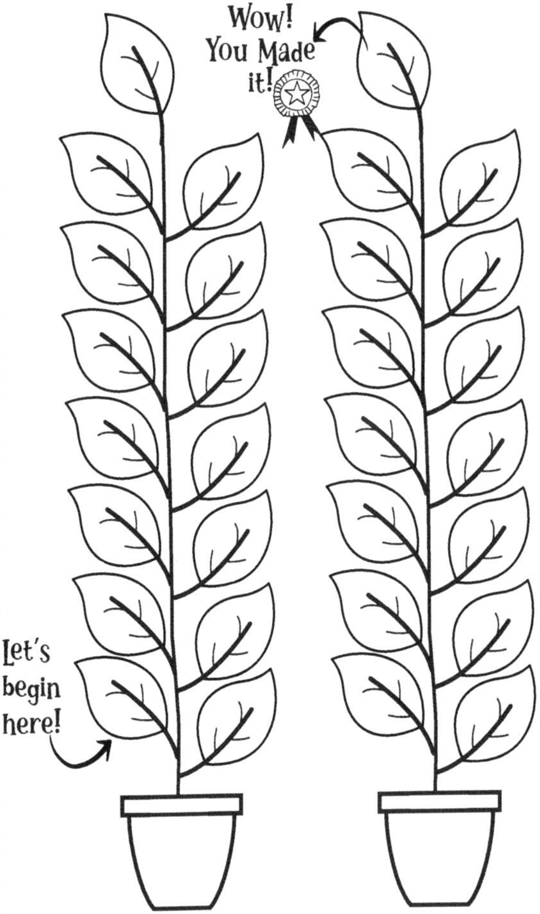

Duration = 30 Days   Goal = $ _ _ _

Start date - . . . .   Finish date - . . . .

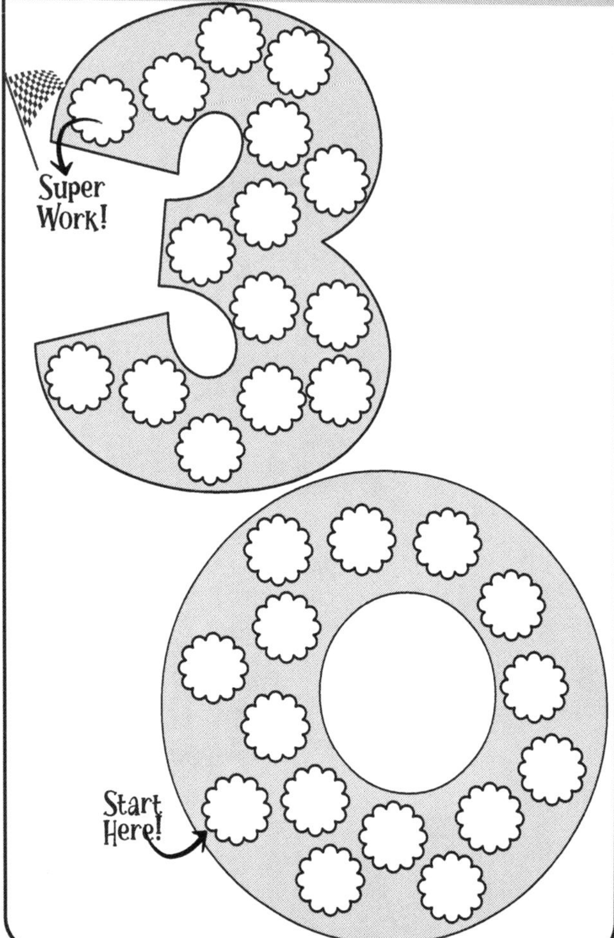

Duration = 30 Days Goal = $ _ _ _

Start date - . . . . Finish date - . . . .

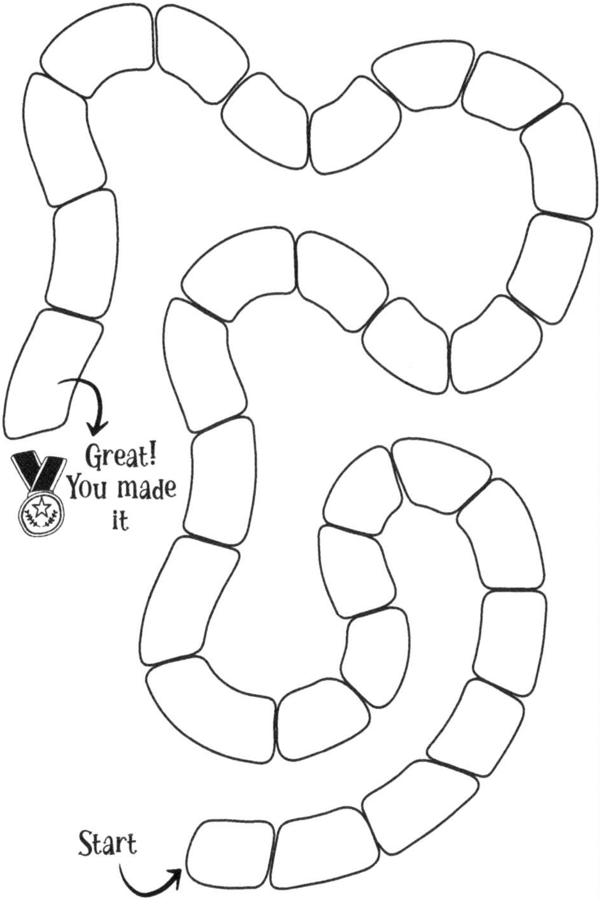

Duration = 30 Days | Goal = $ _ _ _

Start date - .... | Finish date - ....

Duration = 30 Days   Goal = $ _ _ _

Start date - . . . .   Finish date - . . . .

Super work there!

Let's begin here!

50 Day Money Saving Challenges

- $1 Savings Challenge (Save $50) - 2 Challenges
- $2 Savings Challenge (Save $100) - 2 Challenges
- $3 Savings Challenge (Save $150) - 2 Challenges
- $4 Savings Challenge (Save $200) - 2 Challenges
- $5 Savings Challenge (Save $250) - 2 Challenges
- $10 Savings Challenge (Save $500) - 2 Challenges
- $15 Savings Challenge (Save $750) - 2 Challenges
- $20 Savings Challenge (Save $1,000) - 2 Challenges
- $25 Savings Challenge (Save $1,250) - 2 Challenges
- $30 Savings Challenge (Save $1,500) - 2 Challenges
- $40 Savings Challenge (Save $2,000) - 2 Challenges
- $50 Savings Challenge (Save $2,500) - 2 Challenges
- Set your own challenge - 4 Challenges*

*** Set your own challenge**
During this challenge you can save any amount or commit to any saving related activity. Depending on the challenge you decide to go forward, simply color in the icons accordingly.

Each challenge has a starting point and a finishing point. However, only in some challenges, you need to follow a specific path, and in others you can choose your own path to reach the finishing point. Once you start a challenge, keep going, do not break, and always try to finish within the given time period.
Per day/week saving amount is the same for some challenges and it is different for other challenges. So, depending on the challenge, choose the amount and save it for a particular week or day. Once you have that amount saved, simply color in the icon on each savings challenge and see your progress!
Happy Saving Journey !

50-Day Savings Challenges

Duration = 50 Days Goal = $ 50

Start date - . . . . Finish date - . . . .

Each step = $ 1

Duration = 50 Days   Goal = $ 50

Start date - . . . .   Finish date - . . . .

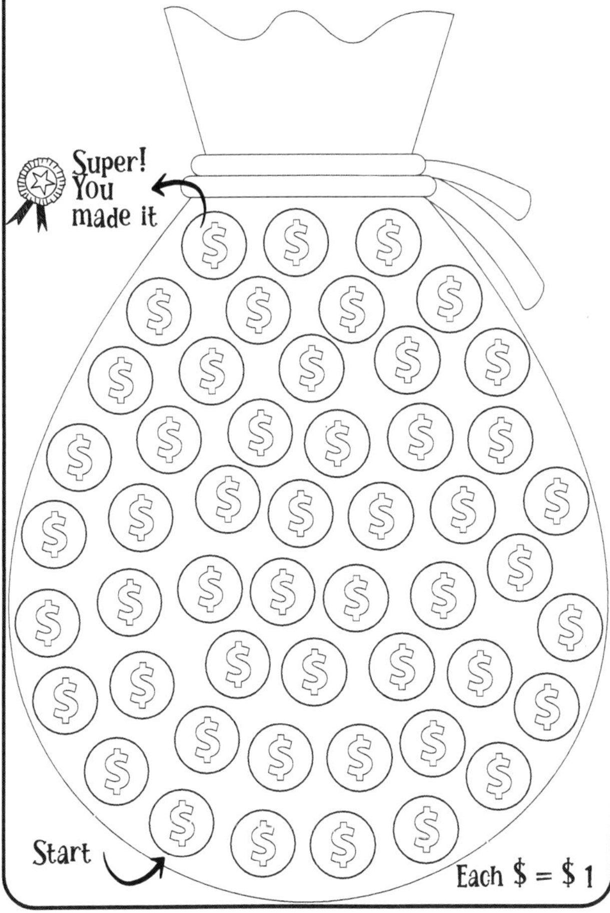

Each $ = $ 1

Duration = 50 Days   Goal = $ 100

Start date - . . . .   Finish date - . . . .

Each Drop = $ 2

Duration = 50 Days

Goal = $ 100

Start date - ....

Finish date - ....

Great! You Did It

Let's take the Start from here!

Each Flower = $ 2

Duration = 50 Days

Goal = $ 150

Start date - . . . .

Finish date - . . . .

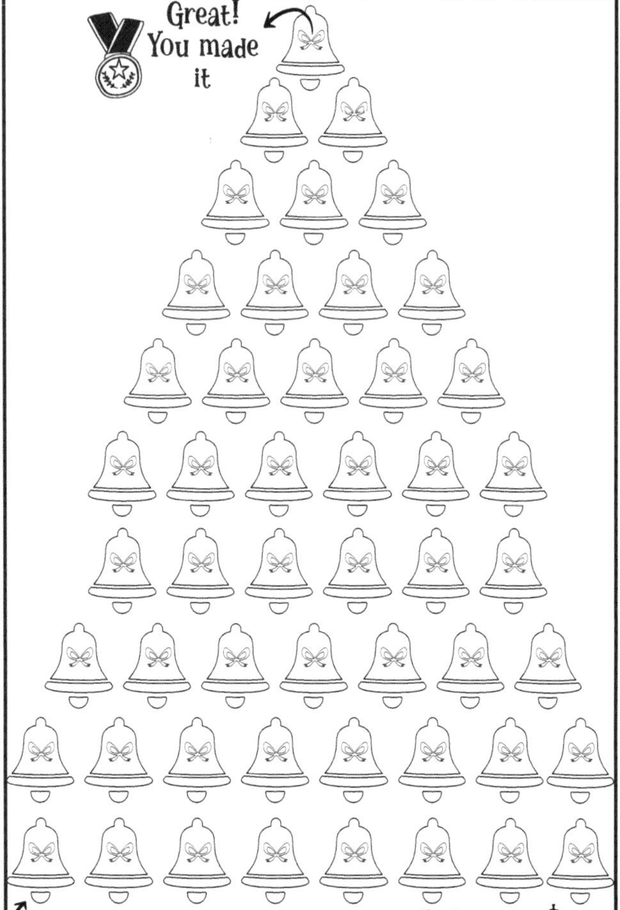

Start

Each Bell = $ 3

Duration = 50 Days | Goal = $ 150

Start date - . . . . | Finish date - . . . .

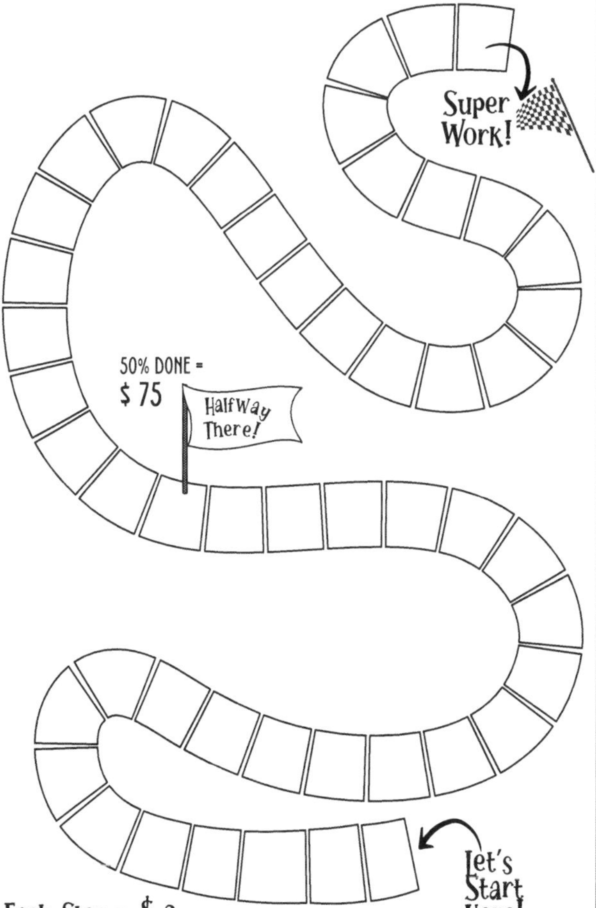

Each Step = $ 3

Duration = 50 Days

Goal = $ 200

Start date - . . . .

Finish date - . . . .

Great Work!

Start

Each Cactus = $ 4

Duration = 50 Days

Goal = $ 200

Start date - . . . .

Finish date - . . . .

You Did It!

Start

Each Egg = $ 4

Duration = 50 Days Goal = $ 250

Start date - .... Finish date - ....

Growing my Money Tree

Each Leaf= $ 5

Duration = 50 Days   Goal = $ 250

Start date - . . . .   Finish date - . . . .

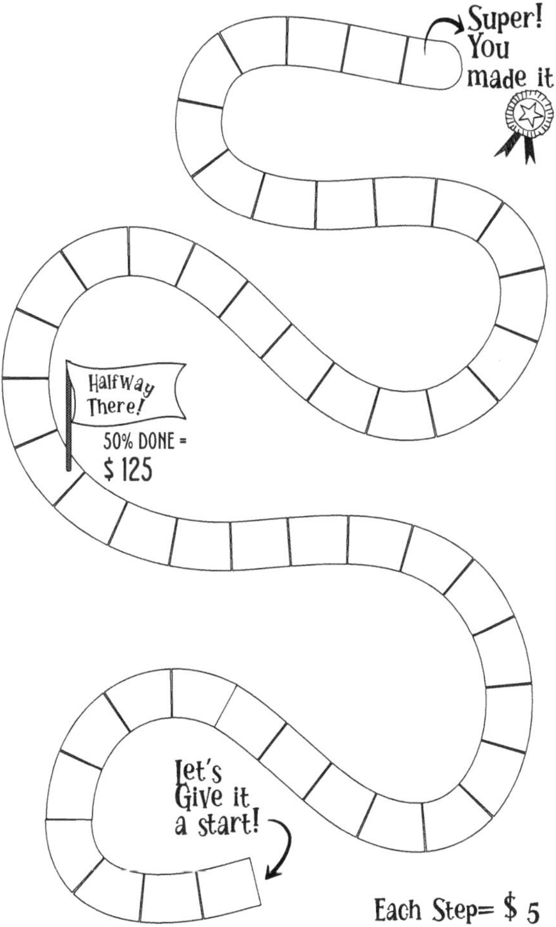

Each Step= $ 5

Duration = 50 Days   Goal = $ 500

Start date - . . . .   Finish date - . . . .

Reach for the Stars

Wow! You Made it!

Start

Each Star = $ 10

Duration = 50 Days | Goal = $ 500

Start date - .... | Finish date - ....

Each rose= $ 10

Duration = 50 Days   Goal = $ 750

Start date - . . . .   Finish date - . . . .

Each heart= $ 15

Duration = 50 Days

Goal = $ 750

Start date - . . . .

Finish date - . . . .

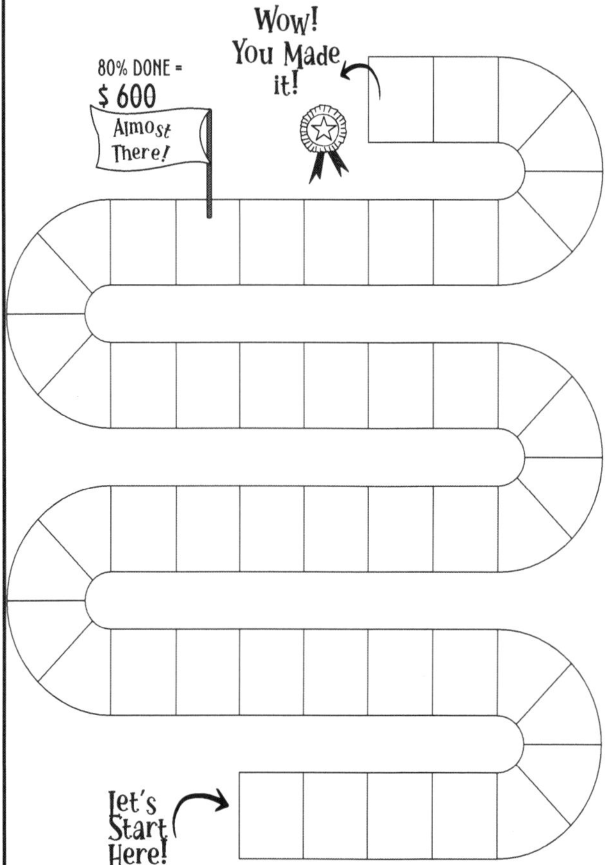

Each Step= $ 15

Duration = 50 Days   Goal = $ 1000

Start date - . . . .   Finish date - . . . .

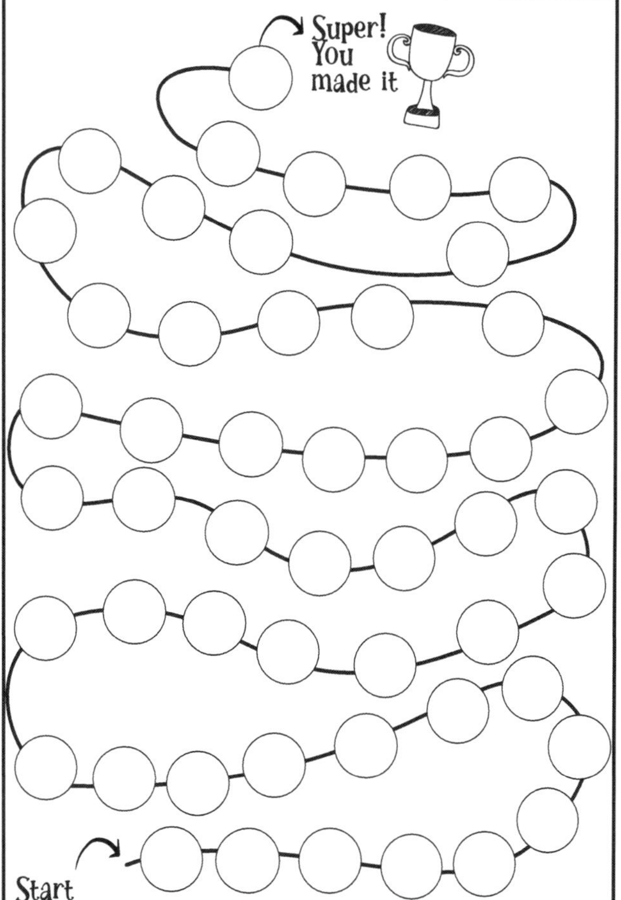

Each circle = $ 20

Duration = 50 Days

Goal = $ 1000

Start date - . . . .

Finish date - . . . .

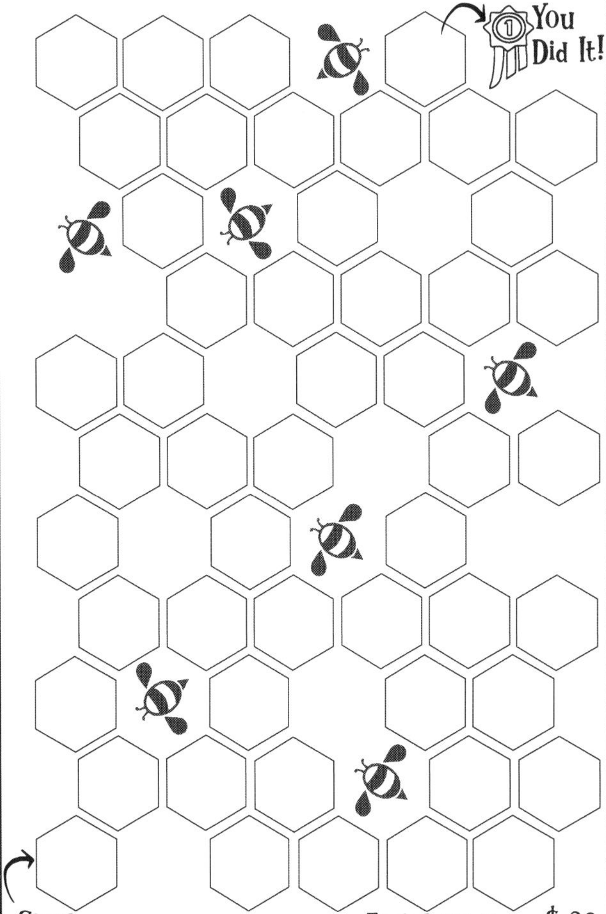

Start

Each hexagon = $ 20

Duration = 50 Days　　Goal = $ 1250

Start date - . . . .　　Finish date - . . . .

Let it Bloom!

Each flower = $ 25

Duration = 50 Days Goal = $ 1250

Start date - . . . . Finish date - . . . .

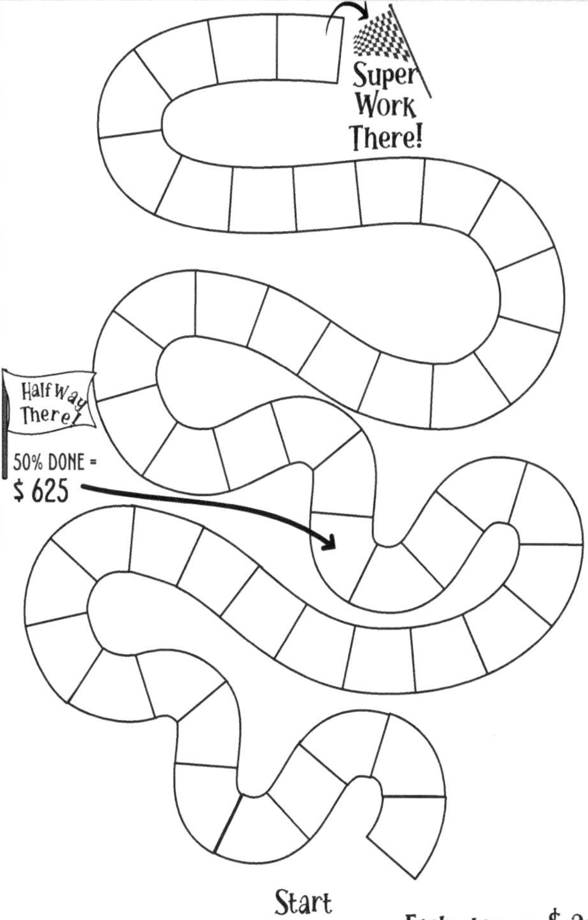

Each step = $ 25

Duration = 50 Days

Goal = $ 1500

Start date - . . . .

Finish date - . . . .

Each heart= $ 30

Duration = 50 Days   Goal = $ 1500

Start date - . . . .   Finish date - . . . .

Awesome! You Did It

Start

Each hive = $ 25

Duration = 50 Days Goal = $ 2000

Start date - . . . . Finish date - . . . .

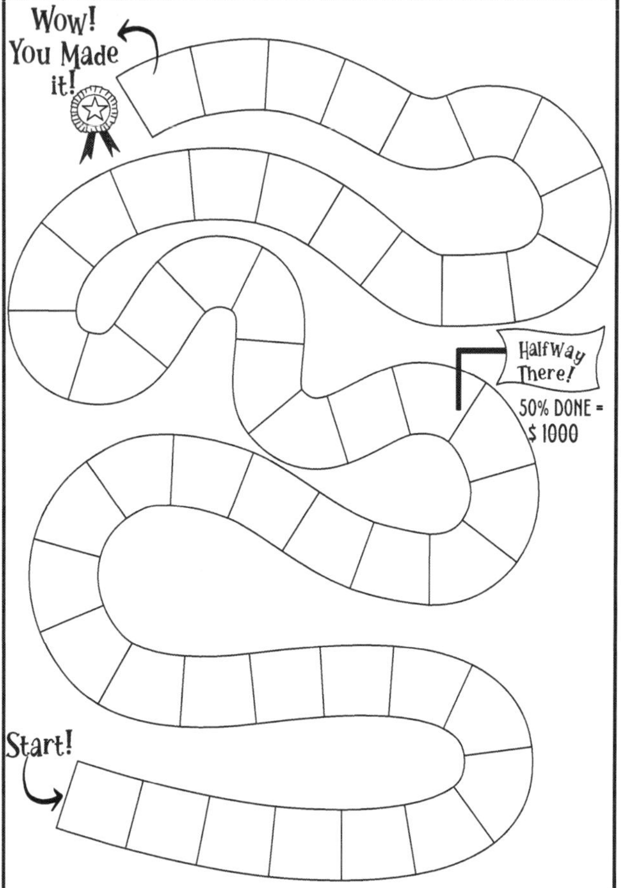

Each step = $ 40

Duration = 50 Days Goal = $ 2000

Start date - . . . . Finish date - . . . .

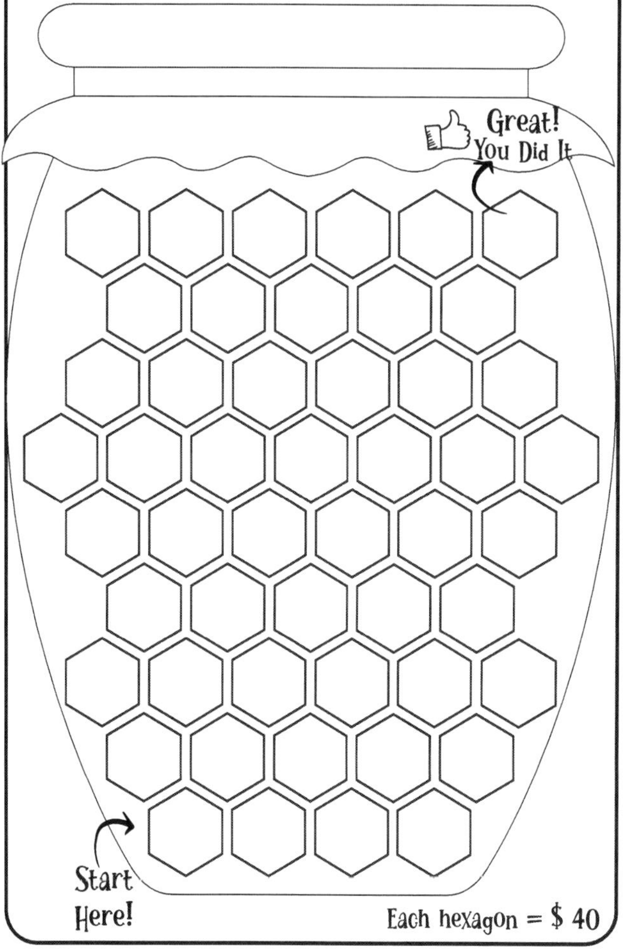

Each hexagon = $ 40

Duration = 50 Days   Goal = $ 2500

Start date - ....   Finish date - ....

Each Piece = $ 50

Duration = 50 Days Goal = $ 2500

Start date - . . . . Finish date - . . . .

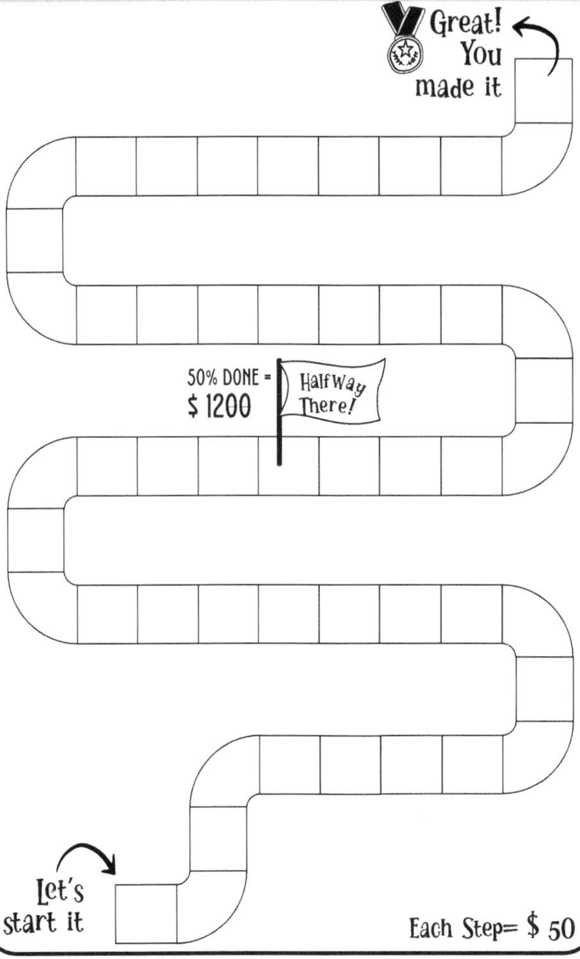

Duration = 50 Days

Goal = $ _ _ _

Start date - . . . .

Finish date - . . . .

Great! You Did It

Start!

Duration = 50 Days | Goal = $ _ _ _

Start date - .... | Finish date - ....

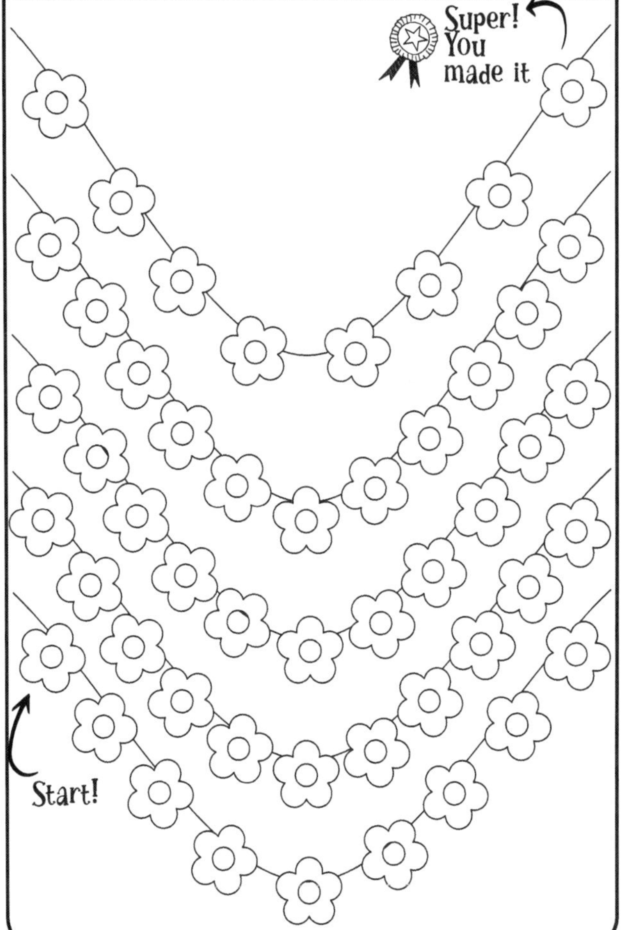

Duration = 50 Days   Goal = $ _ _ _

Start date - . . . .   Finish date - . . . .

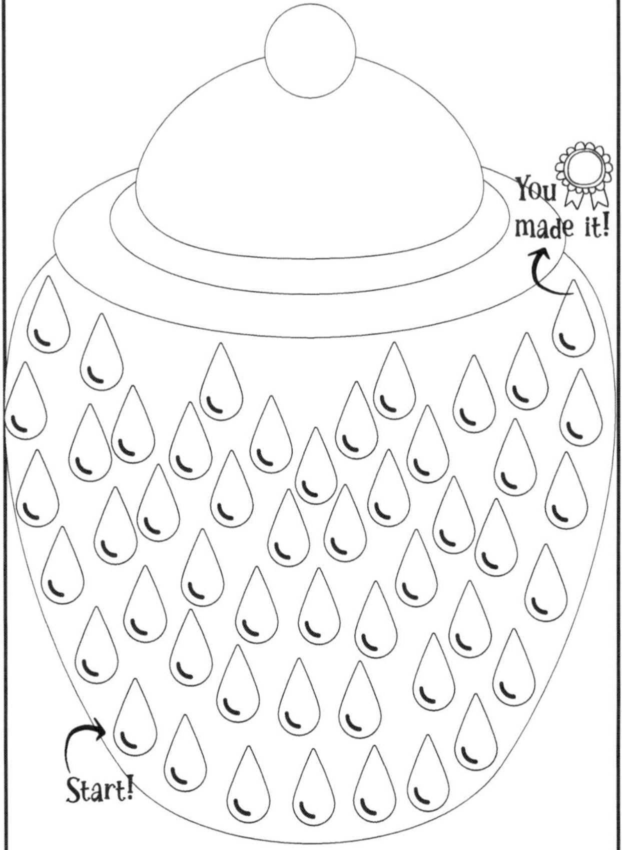

Duration = 50 Days Goal = $ _ _ _

Start date - .... Finish date - ....

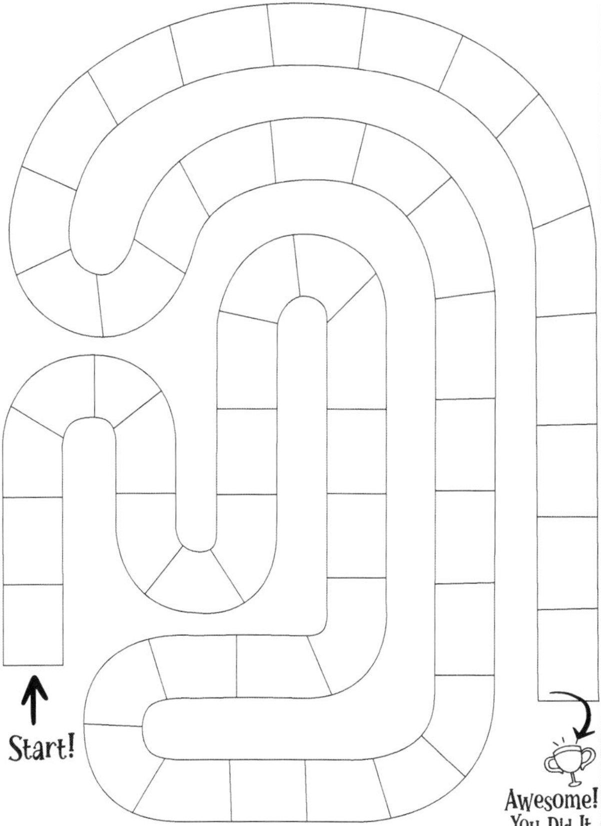

Start!

Awesome! You Did It

100 Days Money Saving Challenges

- $500 Saving Challenge - 2 Challenges
- $1000 Saving Challenge - 2 Challenges
- $5000 Savings Challenge - 2 Challenges
- Set your own challenge - 4 Challenges*

*** Set your own challenge**
During this challenge you can save any amount or commit to any saving related activity. Depending on the challenge you decide to go forward, simply color in the icons accordingly.

Each challenge has a starting point and a finishing point. However, only in some challenges, you need to follow a specific path, and in others you can choose your own path to reach the finishing point. Once you start a challenge, keep going, do not break, and always try to finish within the given time period.
Per day/week saving amount is the same for some challenges and it is different for other challenges. So, depending on the challenge, choose the amount and save it for a particular week or day. Once you have that amount saved, simply color in the icon on each savings challenge and see your progress!

Happy Saving Journey !

100-Day Savings Challenges

Duration = 100 Days

Goal = $ 500

Start date - . . . .

Finish date - . . . .

Each leaf = $ 5

Duration = 100 Days Goal = $ 500

Start date - . . . . Finish date - . . . .

Reach for the Stars

Start

Each star = $ 5

Duration = 100 Days   Goal = $ 1000

Start date - . . . .   Finish date - . . . .

Each heart = $ 10

Duration = 100 Days Goal = $ 1000

Start date - . . . . Finish date - . . . .

Awesome! You Did It

Let's start here

Each rose = $ 10

Duration = 100 Days

Goal = $ 5000

Start date - . . . .

Finish date - . . . .

Wow! You Made it!

Each hexagon = $ 50

Start

Duration = 100 Days   Goal = $ 5000

Start date - . . . .   Finish date - . . . .

Each drop = $ 50

Duration = 100 Days

Goal = $ _ _ _

Start date - . . . .

Finish date - . . . .

Wow!
You Made it!

Start

Duration = 100 Days   Goal = $ _ _ _

Start date - . . . .   Finish date - . . . .

Great! You Did It

Start

Duration = 100 Days   Goal = $ _ _ _

Start date - . . . .   Finish date - . . . .

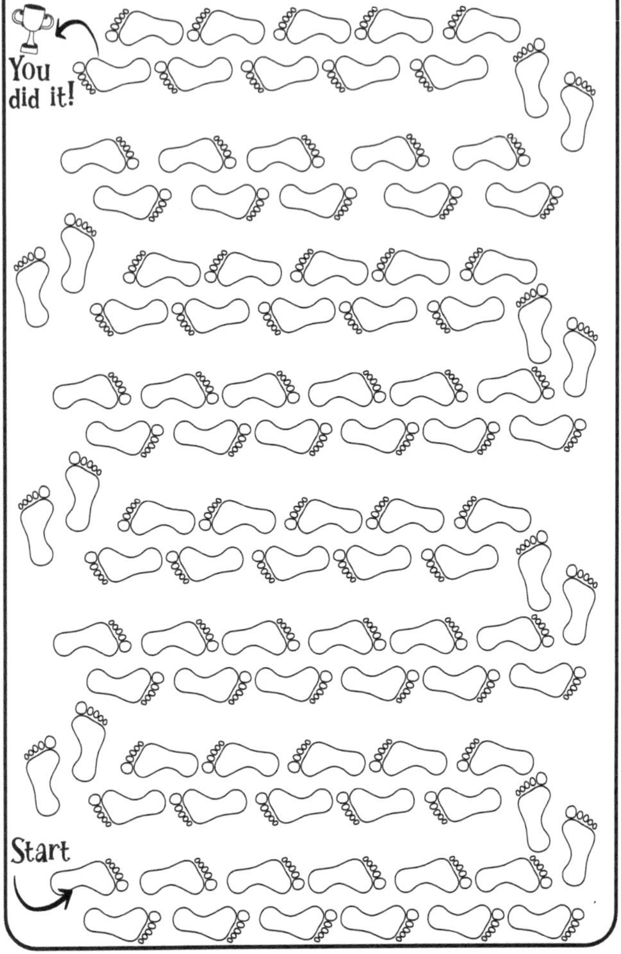

Duration = 100 Days Goal = $ _ _ _

Start date - . . . . Finish date - . . . .

26 Week Money Saving Challenges

- +$ 1 Forward Saving Challenge (Save $351) - 2 Challenges
- -$ 1 Backward Saving Challenge (Save $351) - 2 Challenges
- +$ 2 Forward Savings Challenge (Save $702) - 2 Challenges
- -$ 2 Backward Savings Challenge (Save $702) - 2 Challenges
- $2000 Saving Challenge - 2 Challenges
- $2500 Savings Challenge - 2 Challenges
- $3000 Savings Challenge - 2 Challenges
- $5000 Savings Challenge - 2 Challenges
- $10000 Savings Challenge - 2 Challenges
- $15000 Savings Challenge - 2 Challenges
- Set your own challenge - 4 Challenges*

*** Set your own challenge**
During this challenge you can save any amount or commit to any saving related activity. Depending on the challenge you decide to go forward, simply color in the icons accordingly.

Each challenge has a starting point and a finishing point. However, only in some challenges, you need to follow a specific path, and in others you can choose your own path to reach the finishing point. Once you start a challenge, keep going, do not break, and always try to finish within the given time period.

Per day/week saving amount is the same for some challenges and it is different for other challenges. So, depending on the challenge, choose the amount and save it for a particular week or day. Once you have that amount saved, simply color in the icon on each savings challenge and see your progress!

Happy Saving Journey !

26-Week Savings Challenges

Duration = 26 Weeks | Goal = $ 351

Start date - .... | Finish date - ....

Growing my Money Tree

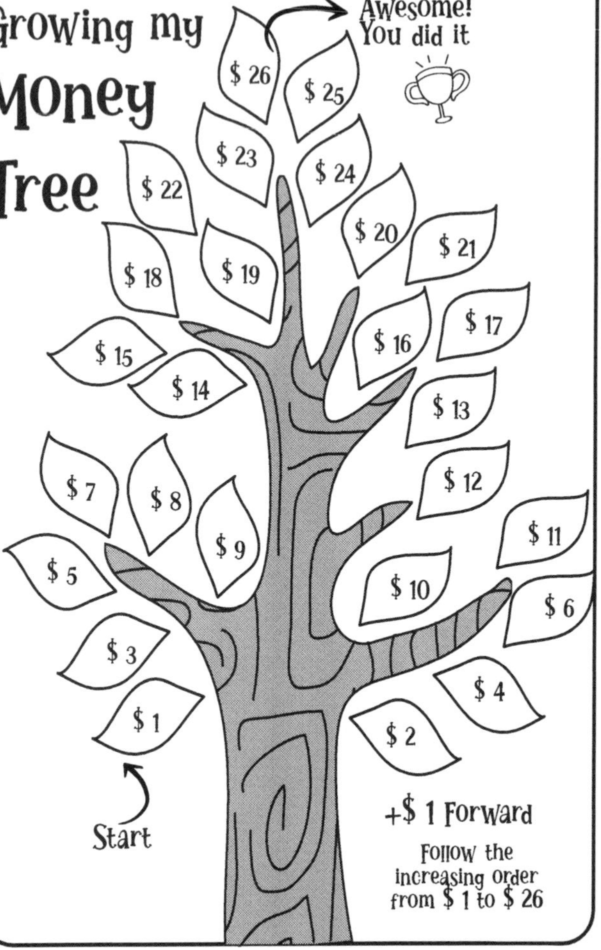

+$ 1 Forward

Follow the increasing order from $ 1 to $ 26

Duration = 26 Weeks Goal = $ 351

Start date - . . . . Finish date - . . . .

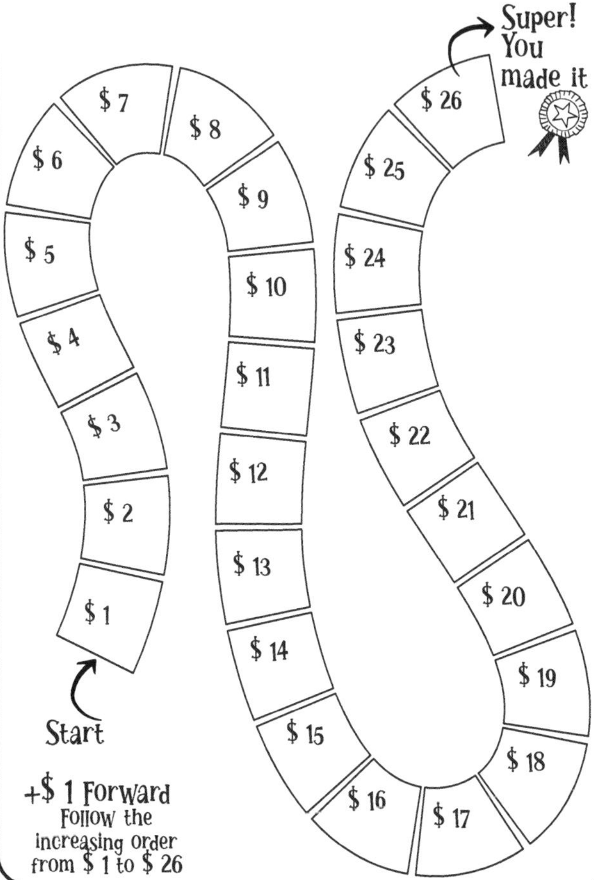

Duration = 26 Weeks | Goal = $ 351

Start date - . . . . Finish date - . . . .

-$ 1 Reverse

Follow the decreasing order from $ 26 to $ 1

Each Drop Counts...

Awesome! You Did It

$ 1

$ 3 $ 2

$ 6 $ 5 $ 4

$ 10 $ 7 $ 8 $ 9

$ 16 $ 11

$ 13 $ 14

$ 12 $ 15

$ 22 $ 17

$ 20

$ 23 $ 18 $ 19

$ 21

$ 26 $ 25 $ 24

Let's start here

Duration = 26 Weeks   Goal = $ 351

Start date - . . . .   Finish date - . . . .

-$ 1 Reverse

Follow the decreasing order from $ 26 to $ 1

Wow! You made it there

Reach for the Stars

$ 1

$ 3 $ 2

$ 4 $ 5

$ 8 $ 7 $ 6

$ 9 $ 10 $ 11 $ 12

$ 16 $ 15 $ 14 $ 13

$ 17 $ 18 $ 19 $ 20 $ 21

$ 26 $ 25 $ 24 $ 23 $ 22

Let's start here

Duration = 26 Weeks   Goal = $ 702

Start date - ....   Finish date - ....

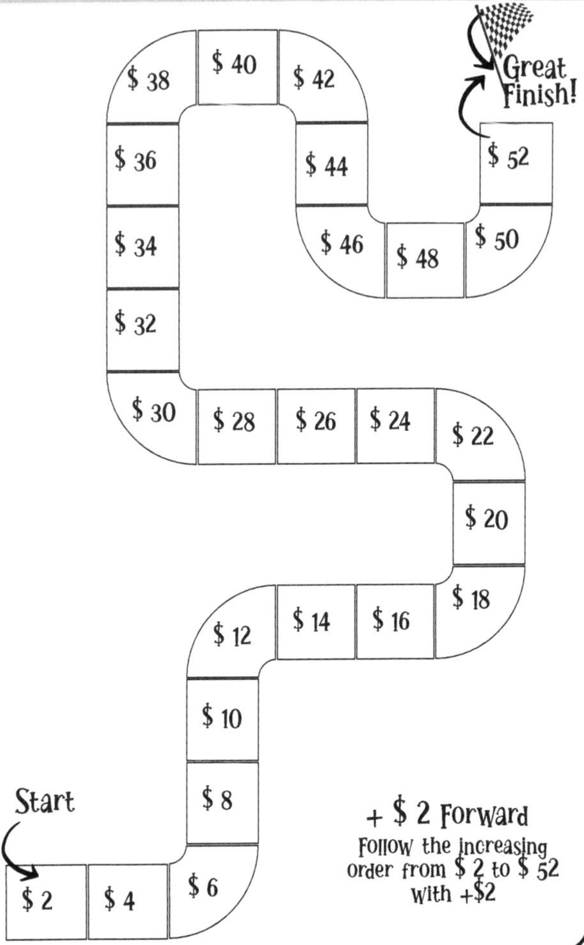

+ $ 2 Forward

Follow the increasing order from $ 2 to $ 52 with +$2

Duration = 26 Weeks

Goal = $ 702

Start date - . . . .

Finish date - . . . .

Great Spirit!

$ 52

$ 50

$ 42

$ 44

$ 46

$ 48

$ 40

$ 38

$ 36

$ 28

$ 30

$ 32

$ 34

$ 26

$ 24

$ 14

$ 16

$ 18

$ 20

$ 22

$ 12

$ 10

$ 2

$ 4

$ 6

$ 8

Start

+ $ 2 Forward

Follow the increasing order from $ 2 to $ 52 with +$2

Duration = 26 Weeks

Goal = $ 702

Start date - ....

Finish date - ....

-$ 2 Reverse

Follow the decreasing order from $ 52 to $ 2 with -$ 2

Duration = 26 Weeks | Goal = $ 702

Start date - .... | Finish date - ....

-$ 2 Reverse

Follow the decreasing order from $ 52 to $ 2 with -$ 2

Duration = 26 Weeks   Goal = $ 2000

Start date - . . . .   Finish date - . . . .

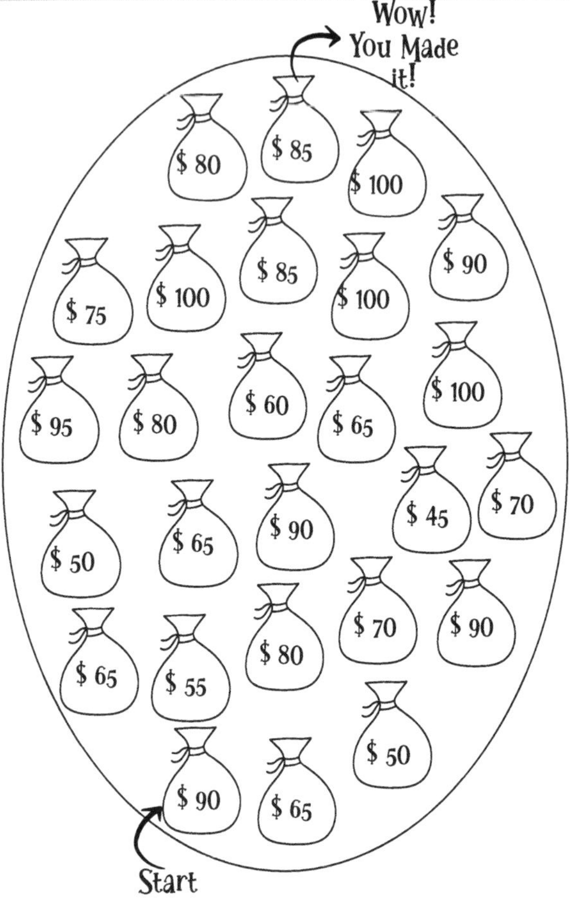

Duration = 26 Weeks   Goal = $ 2000

Start date - . . . .   Finish date - . . . .

Duration = 26 Weeks Goal = $ 2500

Start date - . . . . Finish date - . . . .

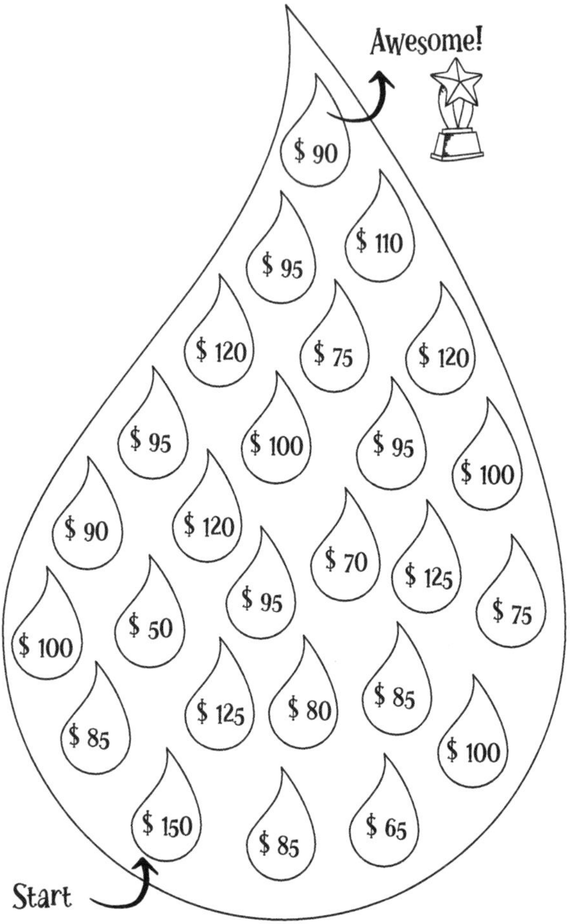

Duration = 26 Weeks | Goal = $ 2500

Start date - . . . . | Finish date - . . . .

Duration = 26 Weeks   Goal = $ 3000

Start date - . . . .   Finish date - . . . .

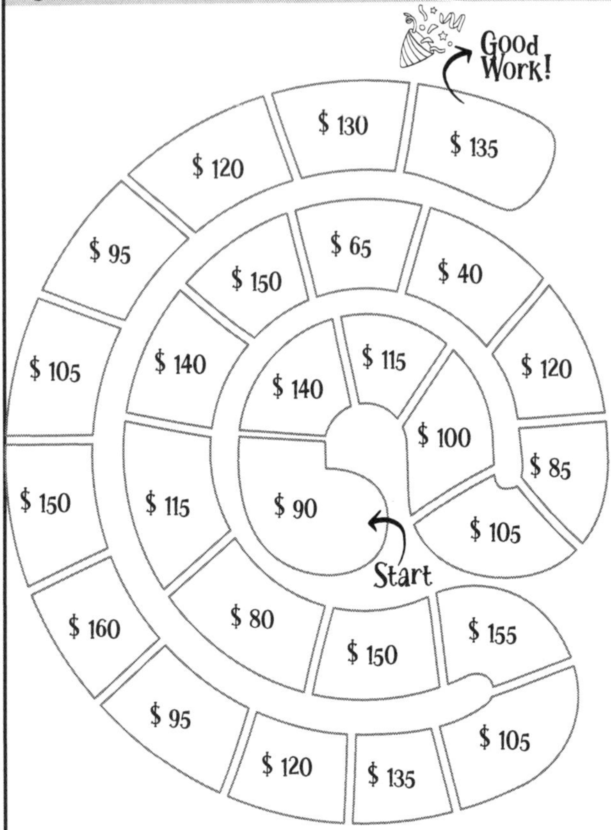

Duration = 26 Weeks

Goal = $ 3000

Start date - . . . .

Finish date - . . . .

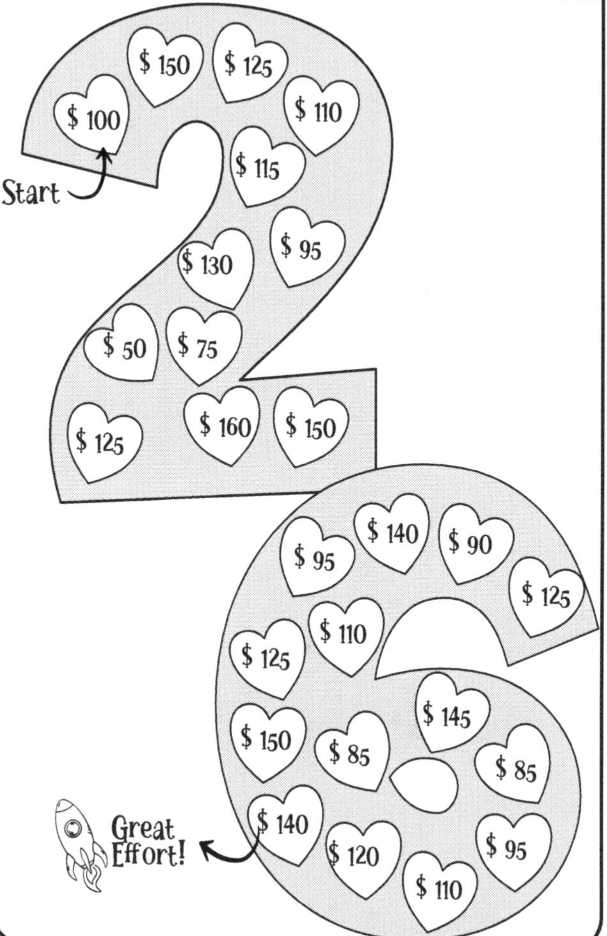

Duration = 26 Weeks Goal = $ 5,000

Start date - . . . . Finish date - . . . .

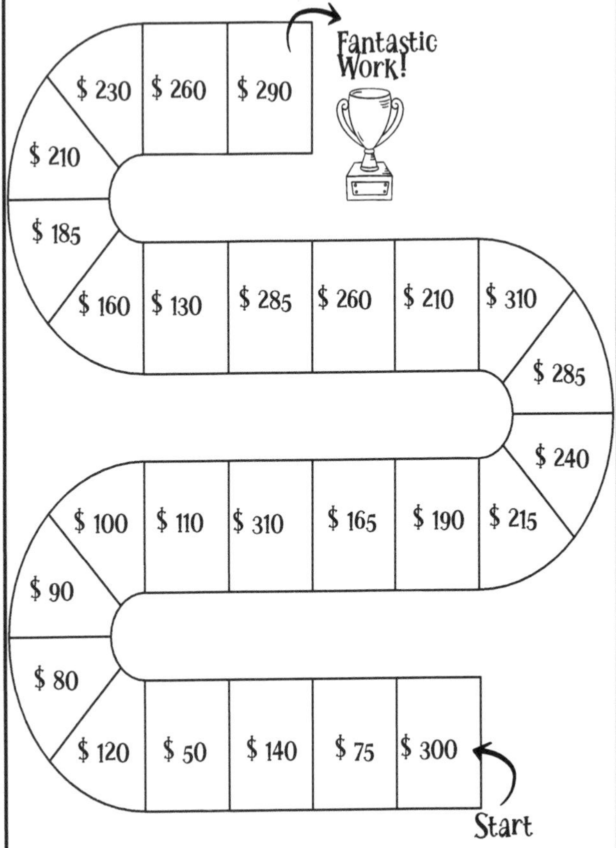

Duration = 26 Weeks | Goal = $ 5,000

Start date - .... | Finish date - ....

Duration = 26 Weeks | Goal = $ 10,000

Start date - . . . . | Finish date - . . . .

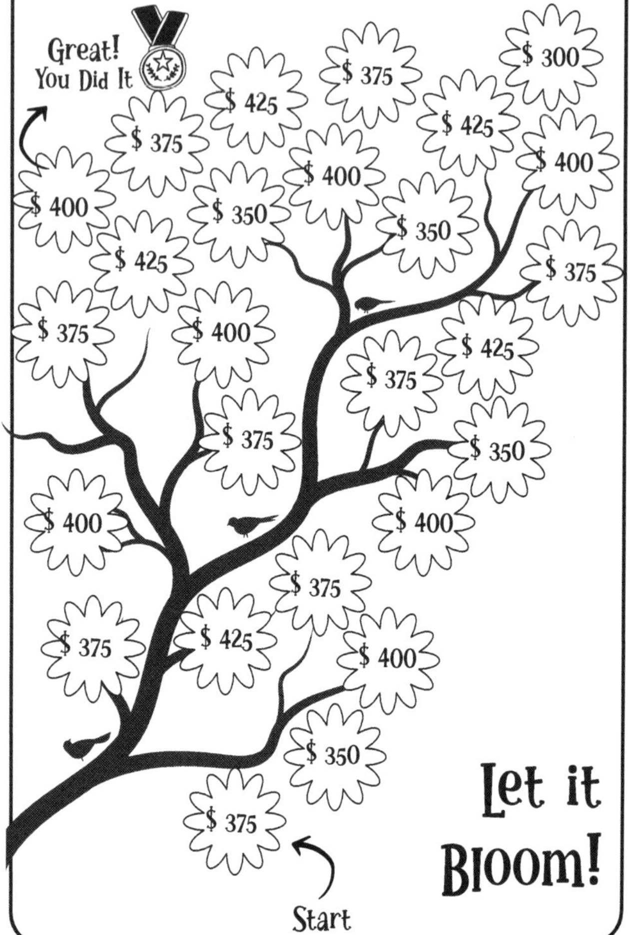

Let it Bloom!

Duration = 26 Weeks   Goal = $ 10,000

Start date - . . . .   Finish date - . . . .

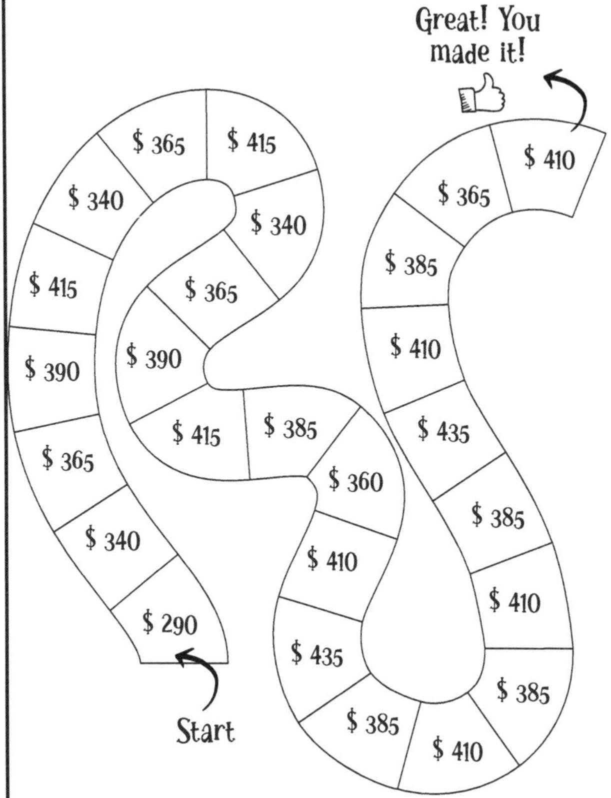

Duration = 26 Weeks   Goal = $ 15,000

Start date - . . . .   Finish date - . . . .

Super Job!

$ 550 | $ 625 | $ 575 | $ 600 | $ 650

$ 750 | $ 650 | $ 550 | $ 625

$ 480 | $ 600 | $ 575 | $ 480 | $ 500

$ 625 | $ 600 | $ 475 | $ 700

$ 710 | $ 550 | $ 575 | $ 650

$ 450 | $ 475 | $ 480 | $ 500

Start

Duration = 26 Weeks

Goal = $ 15,000

Start date - . . . .

Finish date - . . . .

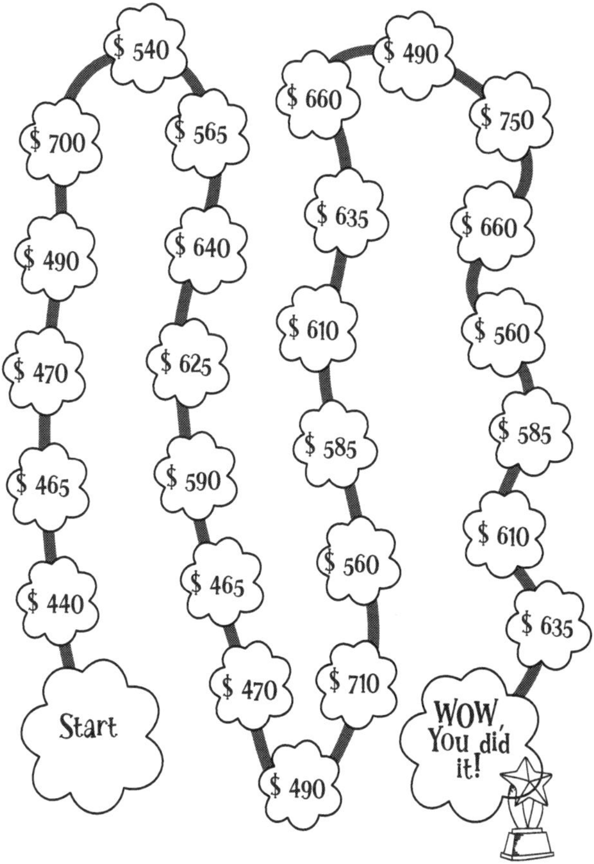

Duration = 26 Weeks Goal = $ _ _ _

Start date - .... Finish date - ....

Duration = 26 Weeks Goal = $ _ _ _

Start date - .... Finish date - ....

Duration = Weeks Goal = $ _ _ _

Start date - .... Finish date - ....

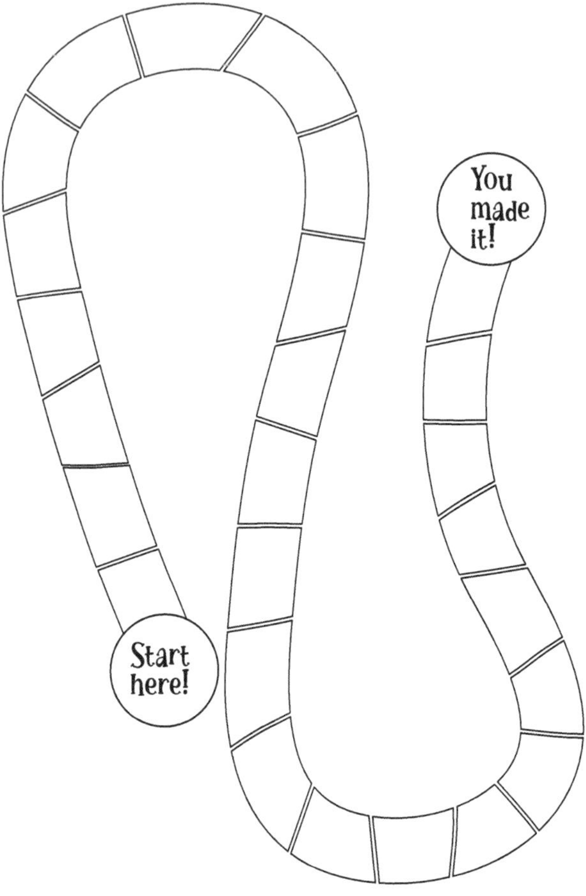

Duration = Weeks Goal = $ _ _ _

Start date - .... Finish date - ....

52 Week Money Saving Challenges

- +$ 1 Forward Saving Challenge (Save $ 1,378) - 2 Challenges
- -$ 1 Backward Saving Challenge (Save $ 1,378) - 2 Challenges
- +$ 2 Forward Savings Challenge (Save $2756) - 2 Challenges
- -$ 2 Backward Savings Challenge (Save $2756) - 2 Challenges
- $2000 Saving Challenge - 2 Challenges
- $2500 Savings Challenge - 2 Challenges
- $3000 Savings Challenge - 2 Challenges
- $5000 Savings Challenge - 2 Challenges
- $6000 Savings Challenge - 2 Challenges
- $10000 Savings Challenge - 2 Challenges
- $15000 Savings Challenge - 2 Challenges
- $20000 Savings Challenge - 2 Challenges
- Set your own challenge - 2 Challenges*

* **Set your own challenge**
During this challenge you can save any amount or commit to any saving related activity. Depending on the challenge you decide to go forward, simply color in the icons accordingly.

Each challenge has a starting point and a finishing point. However, only in some challenges, you need to follow a specific path, and in others you can choose your own path to reach the finishing point. Once you start a challenge, keep going, do not break, and always try to finish within the given time period.
Per day/week saving amount is the same for some challenges and it is different for other challenges. So, depending on the challenge, choose the amount and save it for a particular week or day. Once you have that amount saved, simply color in the icon on each savings challenge and see your progress!
Happy Saving Journey !

52-Week Savings Challenges

Duration = 52 Weeks Goal = $ 1,378

Start date - .... Finish date - ....

+$ 1 Forward : Follow the increasing order from $ 1 to $ 52

$ 47 $ 48 $ 49 $ 50 $ 51 $ 52

Great Job!

$ 46 $ 45 $ 44 $ 43 $ 42

$ 38 $ 39 $ 40 $ 41

$ 37 $ 36 $ 35 $ 34 $ 33 $ 32

$ 28 $ 29 $ 30 $ 31

$ 27 $ 26 $ 25 $ 24 $ 23

$ 19 $ 20 $ 21 $ 22

$ 18 $ 17 $ 16 $ 15 $ 14

$ 11 $ 12 $ 13

$ 10 $ 9 $ 8 $ 7 $ 6 $ 5

$ 1 $ 2 $ 3 $ 4

Start

Duration = 52 Weeks Goal = $ 1,378

Start date - . . . . Finish date - . . . .

+$ 1 Forward : Follow the increasing order from $ 1 to $ 52

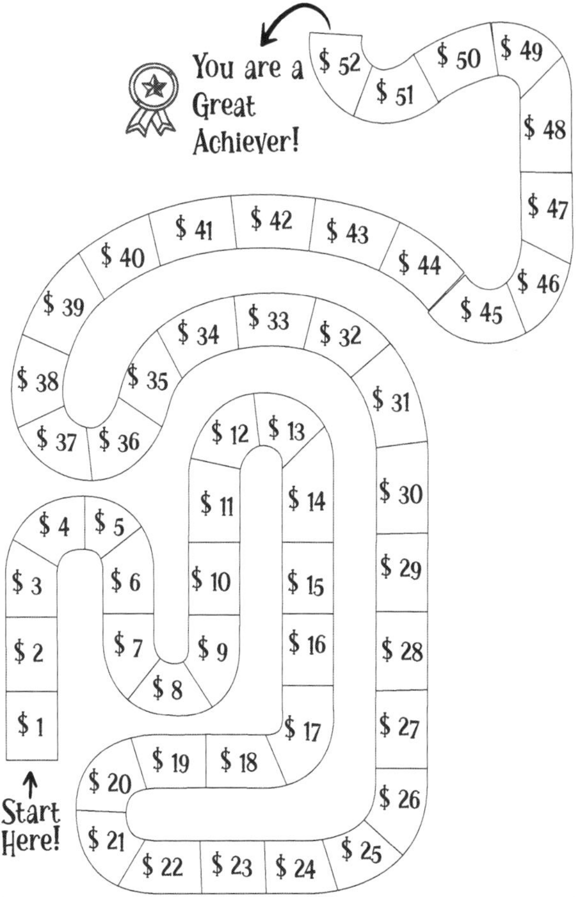

Duration = 52 Weeks　Goal = $ 1,378

Start date - . . . .　Finish date - . . . .

Growing my Money Tree

- $1 Reverse

Follow the decreasing order from $ 52 to $ 1

Duration = 52 Weeks Goal = $ 1,378

Start date - .... Finish date - ....

Each Drop Counts...

- $1 Reverse

Follow the decreasing order from $ 52 to $ 1

Great! You Did It

$ 1

$ 2 $ 3

$ 4

$ 6 $ 5

$ 10 $ 7 $ 9 $ 8

$ 11 $ 12 $ 15 $ 14 $ 13

$ 17 $ 16 $ 18 $ 19 $ 20 $ 21

$ 22 $ 23 $ 24 $ 25 $ 26 $ 27

$ 33 $ 32 $ 31 $ 30 $ 29 $ 28

$ 34 $ 36 $ 37 $ 38 $ 39 $ 40

$ 35 $ 47 $ 46 $ 45 $ 43 $ 41

$ 52 $ 44 $ 42

$ 51 $ 50 $ 49 $ 48

Start

Duration = 52 Weeks | Goal = $ 2,756

Start date - . . . . | Finish date - . . . .

+$ 2 Forward

Follow the increasing order from $ 2 to $ 104

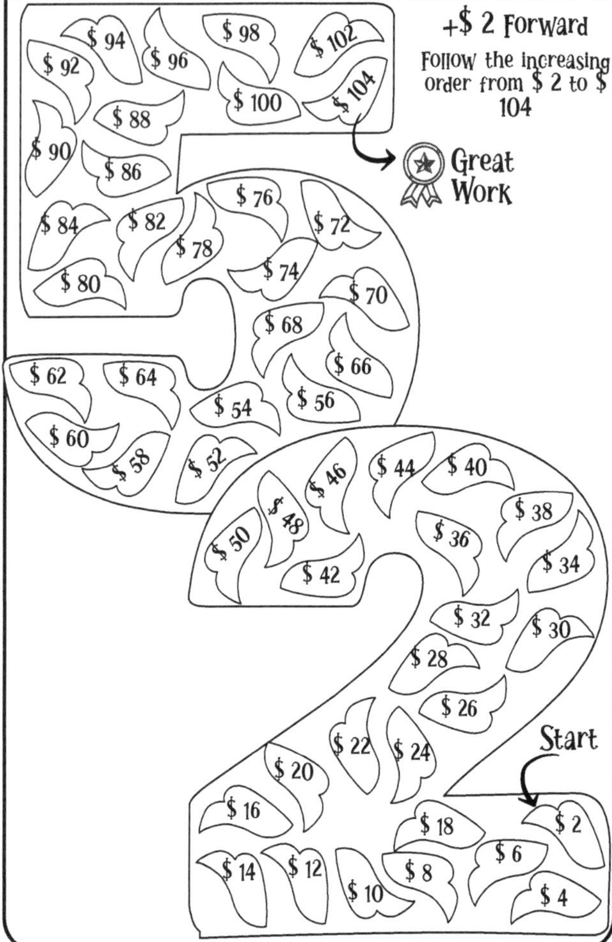

Duration = 52 Weeks   Goal = $ 2,756

Start date - . . . .   Finish date - . . . .

+$ 2 Forward

Follow the increasing order from $ 2 to $ 104

Awesome! You Did It

Start

$ 2 | $ 4 | $ 6 | $ 8 | $ 10 | $ 12 | $ 14 | $ 16 | $ 18 | $ 20 | $ 22 | $ 24 | $ 26 | $ 28 | $ 30 | $ 32 | $ 34 | $ 36 | $ 38 | $ 40 | $ 42 | $ 44 | $ 46 | $ 48 | $ 50 | $ 52 | $ 54 | $ 56 | $ 58 | $ 60 | $ 62 | $ 64 | $ 66 | $ 68 | $ 70 | $ 72 | $ 74 | $ 76 | $ 78 | $ 80 | $ 82 | $ 84 | $ 86 | $ 88 | $ 90 | $ 92 | $ 94 | $ 96 | $ 98 | $ 100 | $ 102 | $ 104

Duration = 52 Weeks   Goal = $ 2,756

Start date - . . . .   Finish date - . . . .

Good Job!

$ 12 $ 10 $ 8 $ 6 $ 4 $ 2

$ 14 $ 16 $ 18 $ 20 $ 22

$ 30 $ 28 $ 26 $ 24

$ 32 $ 34 $ 36

$2 Reverse

Follow the decreasing order from $ 104 to $ 2

$ 40 $ 38

$ 42 $ 44 $ 46

$ 58 $ 56 $ 54 $ 52 $ 50 $ 48

$ 60 $ 62 $ 64

$ 68 $ 66

$ 70 $ 72 $ 74

$ 82 $ 80 $ 78 $ 76

Start

$ 84 $ 86 $ 88 $ 90 $ 92

$ 104 $ 102 $ 100 $ 98 $ 96 $ 94

Duration = 52 Weeks Goal = $ 2,756

Start date - . . . . Finish date - . . . .

- **$2 Reverse** : Follow the decreasing order from $ 104 to $ 2

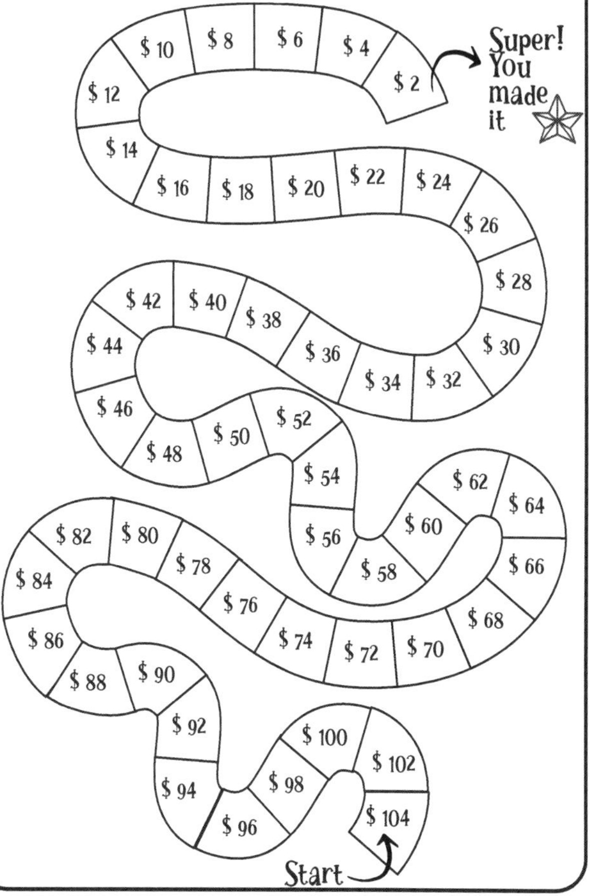

Duration = 52 Weeks Goal = $ 2,000

Start date - . . . . Finish date - . . . .

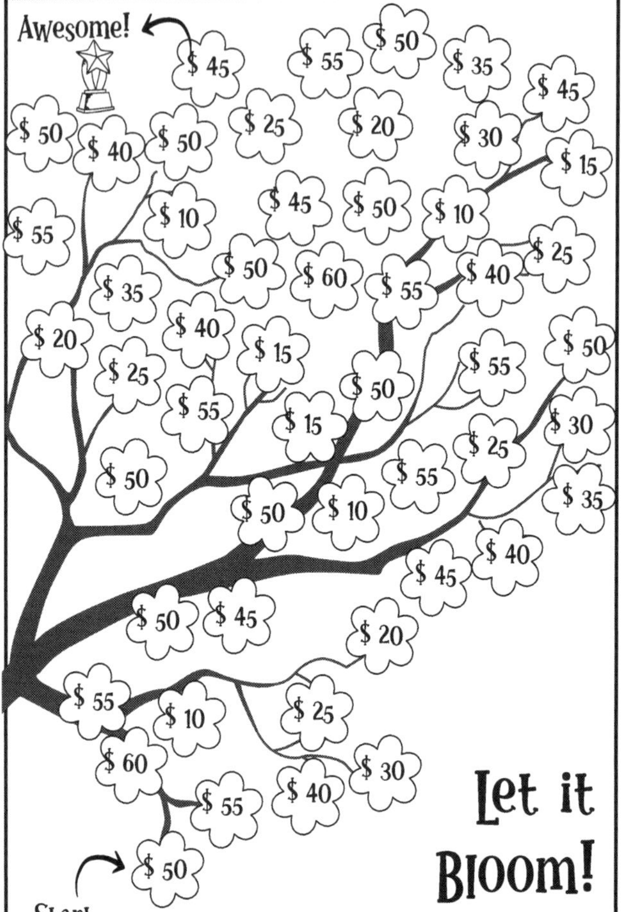

Let it Bloom!

Duration = 52 Weeks

Goal = $ 2,000

Start date - . . . .

Finish date - . . . .

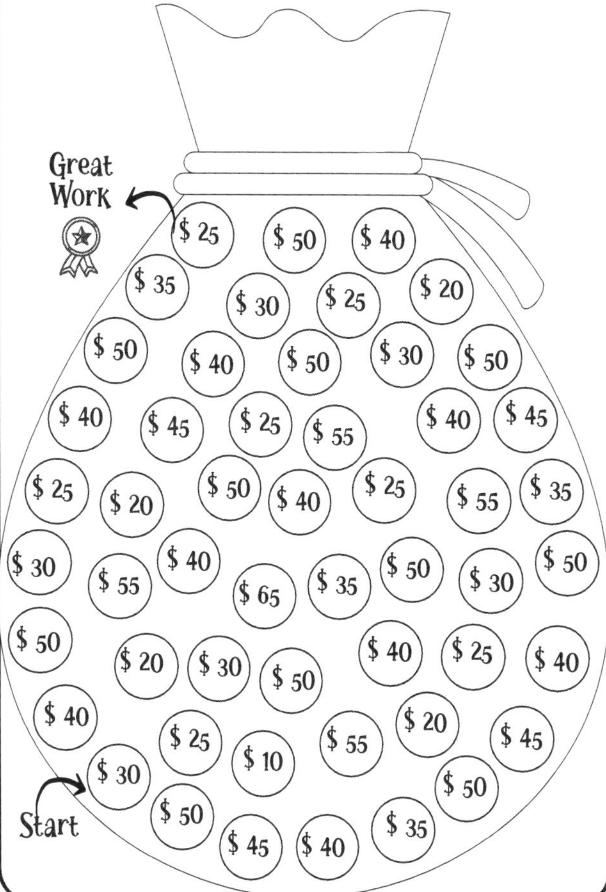

Duration = 52 Weeks Goal = $ 2,500

Start date - . . . . Finish date - . . . .

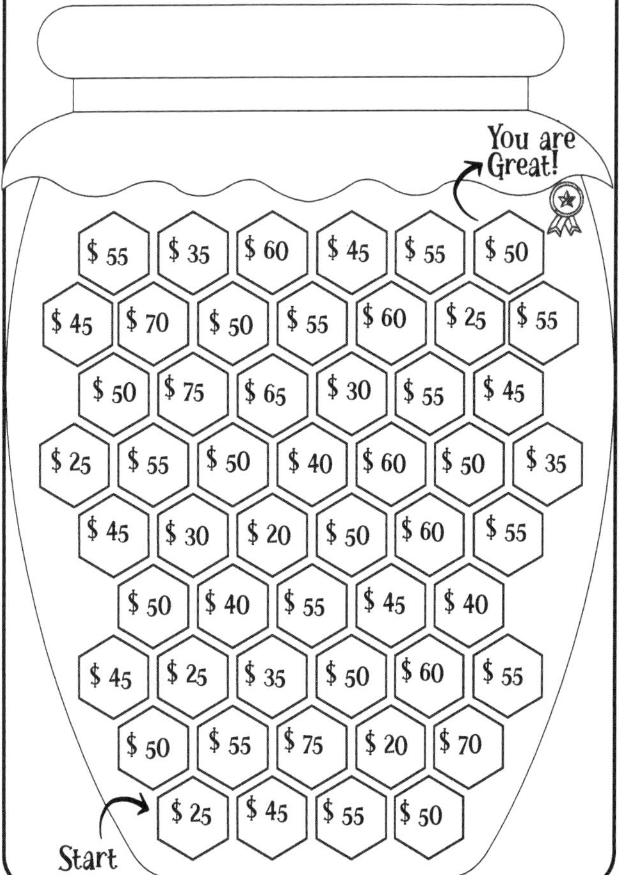

Duration = 52 Weeks Goal = $ 2,500

Start date - . . . . Finish date - . . . .

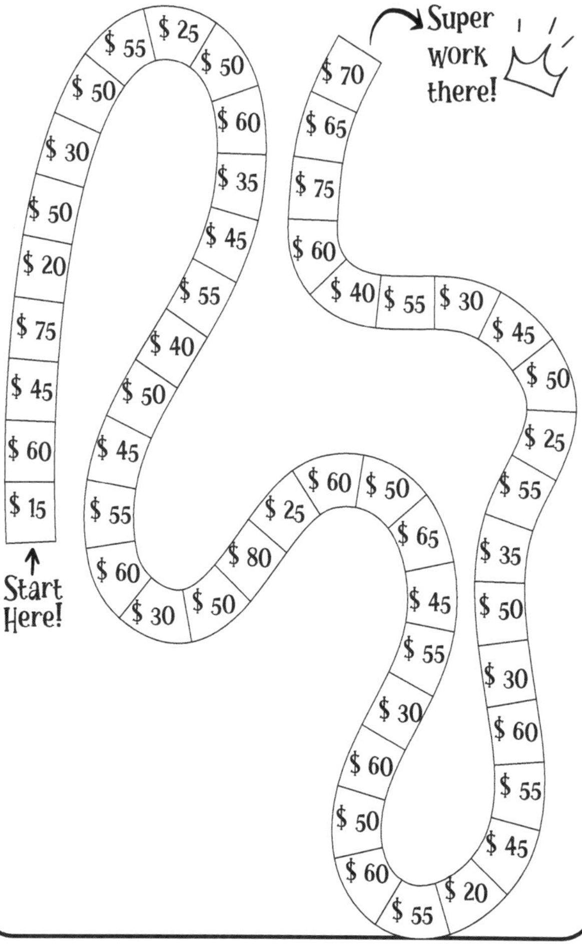

Duration = 52 Weeks　　Goal = $ 3,000

Start date - . . . .　　Finish date - . . . .

Awesome! You made it

$ 75

$ 65　$ 50

$ 45　$ 70　$ 75

$ 60　$ 40　$ 65　$ 40

$ 50　$ 70　$ 60　$ 45　$ 75

$ 65　$ 40　$ 55　$ 50　$ 60　$ 85

$ 45　$ 60　$ 70　$ 60　$ 40　$ 80　$ 55

$ 55　$ 75　$ 50　$ 40　$ 65　$ 70　$ 45　$ 60

$ 45　$ 55　$ 60　$ 50　$ 70　$ 40　$ 60　$ 65

$ 35　$ 75　$ 50　$ 60　$ 45　$ 55　$ 75　$ 50

Start

Duration = 52 Weeks   Goal = $ 3,000

Start date - . . . .   Finish date - . . . .

$ 75 $ 40 $ 65 $ 90 $ 55   Great Work

$ 60 $ 30 $ 45 $ 40 $ 70 $ 75

$ 75 $ 65 $ 55 $ 50 $ 80 $ 65

$ 35 $ 75 $ 45 $ 70 $ 40 $ 75

$ 70 $ 50 $ 75 $ 30 $ 90 $ 65

$ 70 $ 40 $ 65 $ 45 $ 70 $ 60

$ 50 $ 45 $ 80 $ 55 $ 35 $ 40

$ 75 $ 20 $ 30 $ 45 $ 95 $ 70

Start $ 65 $ 25 $ 75 $ 50 $ 40

Duration = 52 Weeks   Goal = $ 5,000

Start date - . . . .   Finish date - . . . .

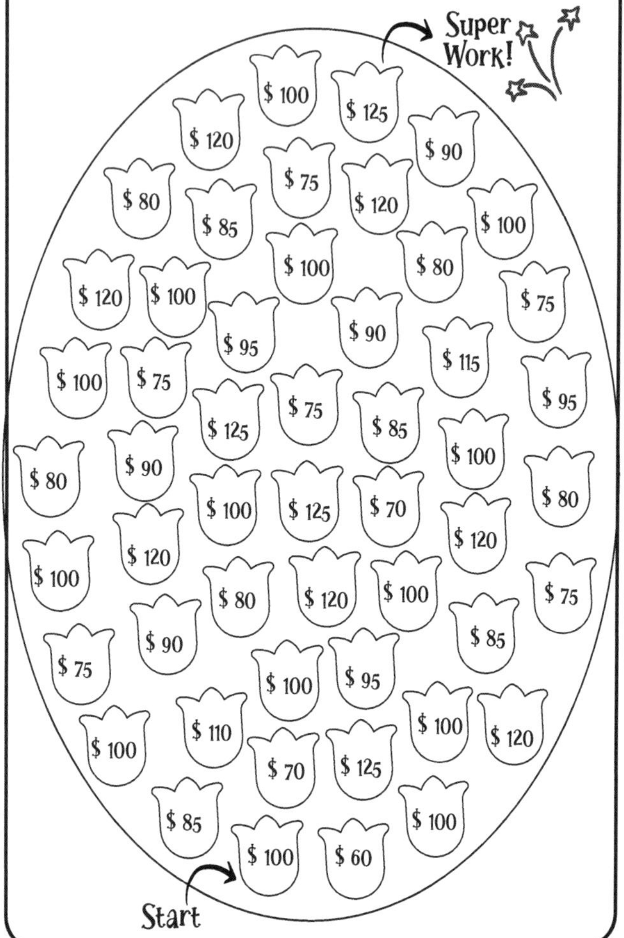

Duration = 52 Weeks

Goal = $ 5,000

Start date - . . . .

Finish date - . . . .

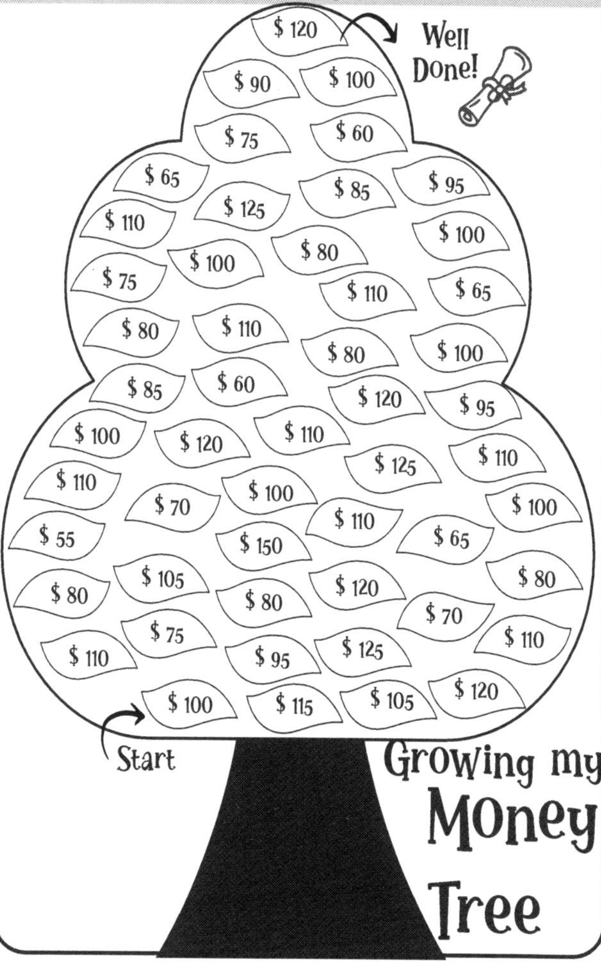

Growing my Money Tree

Duration = 52 Weeks
Goal = $ 6,000
Start date - . . . .
Finish date - . . . .

Duration = 52 Weeks

Goal = $ 6,000

Start date - . . . .

Finish date - . . . .

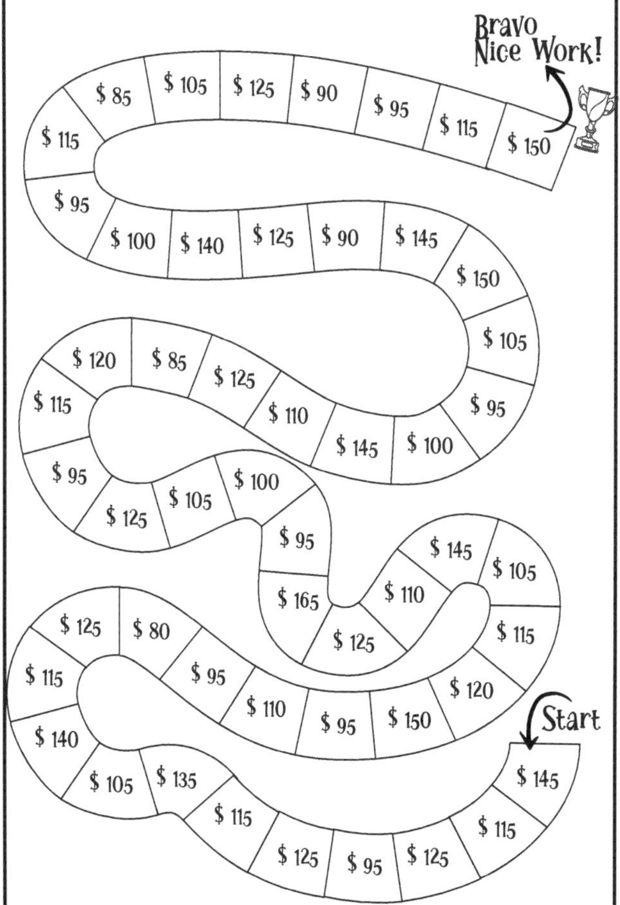

Duration = 52 Weeks   Goal = $ 10,000

Start date - . . . .   Finish date - . . . .

Fantastic Work!

$ 245 $ 150 $ 115

$ 110 $ 145 $ 120 $ 240

$ 220 $ 125 $ 250

$ 200 $ 140

$ 150 $ 210 $ 235 $ 210

$ 155 $ 230 $ 165 $ 255

$ 250 $ 255

$ 185

$ 125 $ 245 $ 115 $ 210 $ 150

$ 145 $ 260

$ 250 $ 240 $ 225

$ 120

$ 140 $ 150 $ 255 $ 155 $ 235

$ 230 $ 250 $ 230

$ 210 $ 200 $ 255 $ 205

$ 150 $ 240 $ 225 $ 145 $ 125 $ 155

Start

Duration = 52 Weeks

Goal = $ 10,000

Start date - . . . .

Finish date - . . . .

Start

$ 150
$ 125
$ 215
$ 220
$ 155
$ 130
$ 200
$ 160
$ 240
$ 170
$ 155
$ 220
$ 225
$ 235
$ 230
$ 240
$ 245
$ 130
$ 250
$ 245
$ 240
$ 165
$ 120
$ 230
$ 200
$ 215
$ 225
$ 125
$ 220
$ 150
$ 160
$ 225
$ 155
$ 210
$ 235
$ 245
$ 170
$ 165
$ 240
$ 220
$ 130
$ 230
$ 245
$ 220
$ 145
$ 190
$ 130
$ 160
$ 125
$ 155
$ 200
$ 215

Awesome!
You Did It

Duration = 52 Weeks Goal = $ 15,000

Start date - . . . . Finish date - . . . .

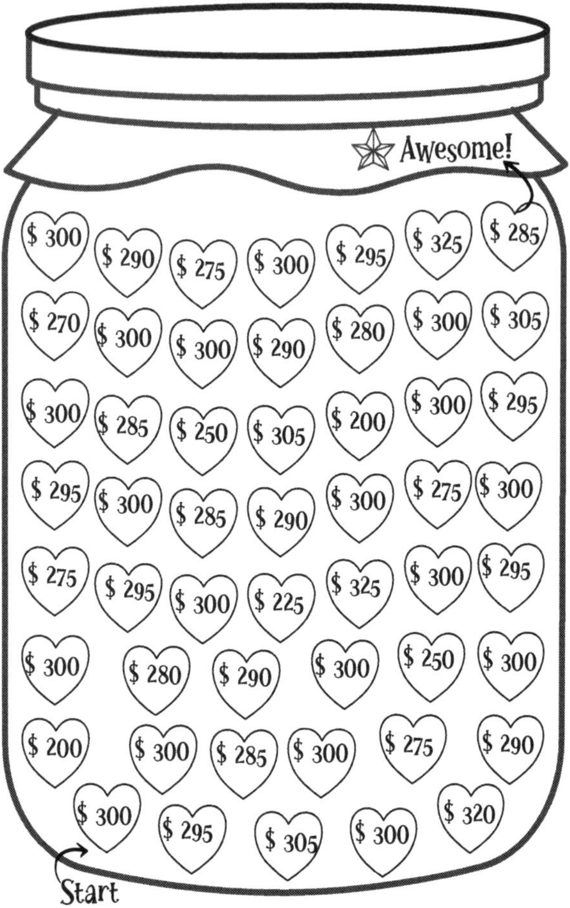

Duration = 52 Weeks

Goal = $ 15,000

Start date - . . . .

Finish date - . . . .

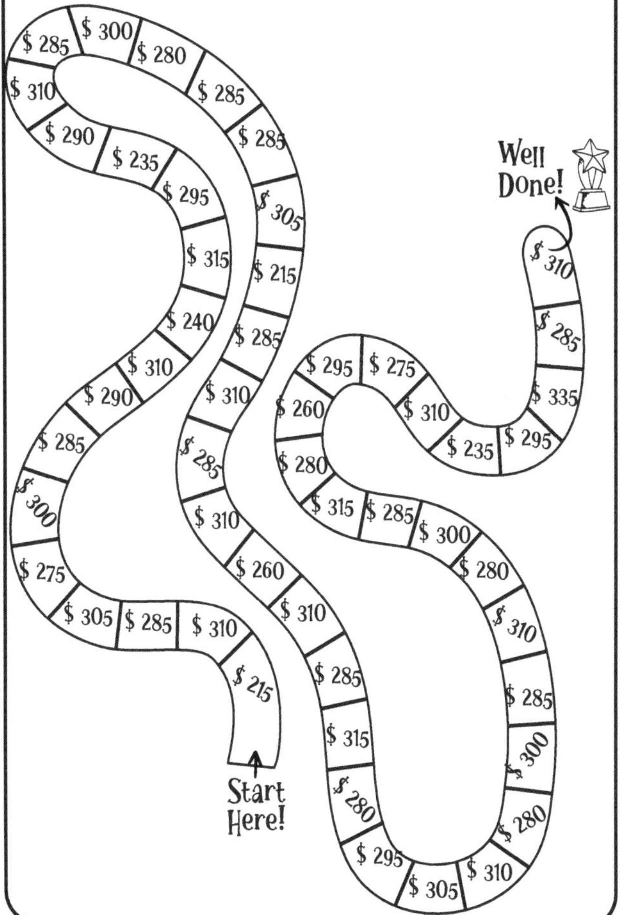

Duration = 52 Weeks Goal = $ 20,000

Start date - . . . . Finish date - . . . .

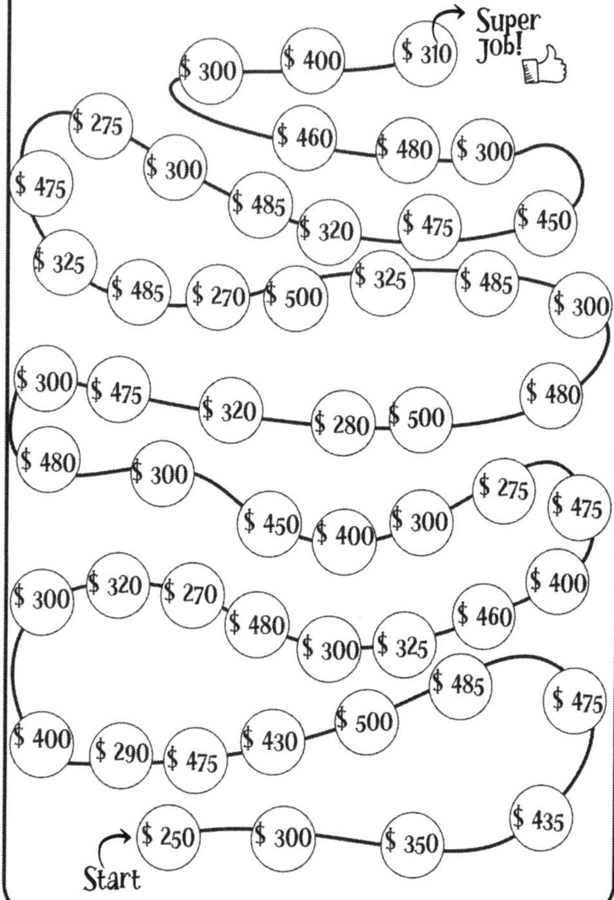

Duration = 52 Weeks   Goal = $ 20,000

Start date - . . . .   Finish date - . . . .

Great! You made it

$ 360 $ 465 $ 310 $ 475 $ 315 $ 240

$ 500 $ 425 $ 520 $ 265 $ 300 $ 310

$ 450 $ 310 $ 465 $ 500

$ 300 $ 490 $ 470

$ 475 $ 310 $ 450 $ 300

$ 300 $ 440 $ 400 $ 465 $ 420 $ 310

$ 310 $ 420 $ 300 $ 315 $ 500 $ 265

$ 500 $ 290 $ 495 $ 310 $ 420 $ 475

$ 470 $ 465 $ 440 $ 330 $ 290

$ 280 $ 450 $ 310 $ 300 $ 465 $ 260

Start

Duration = 52 Weeks   Goal = $ _ _ _

Start date - . . . .   Finish date - . . . .

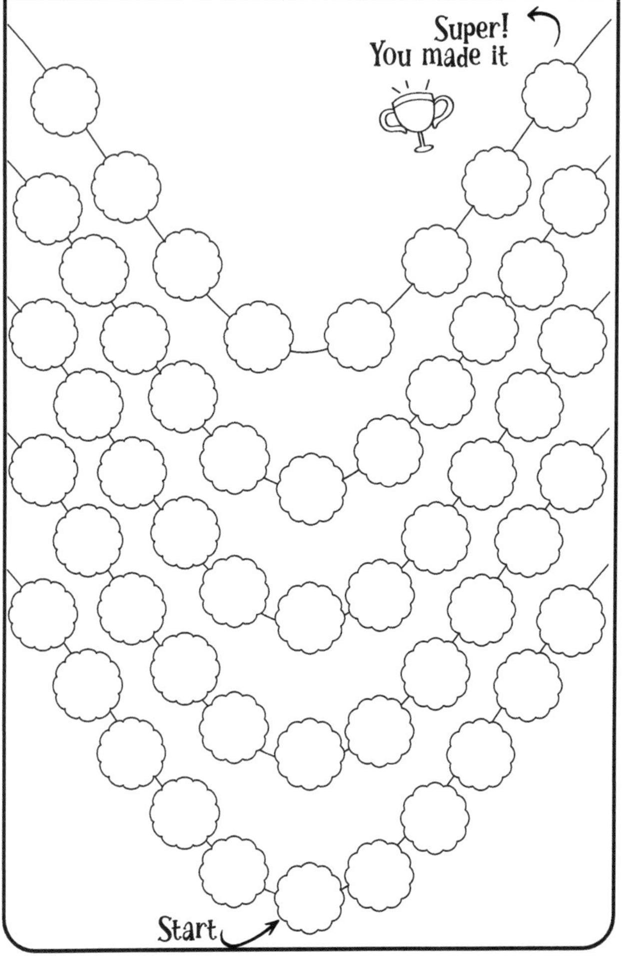

Duration = 52 Weeks Goal = $ _ _ _

Start date - .... Finish date - ....

Reach for the Stars

Awesome! You Did It

Start

Thank you for this purchase from Aurora Publishing

Hope you enjoy this Awesome Savings Book of variety of Money Saving Challenges

Please let us know how you like it!

Positive ratings, reviews and constructive suggestions from awesome people like you help others to feel confident about choosing this book and help us to continue providing great books.

Share your happy experience online in Amazon with the following three steps;

- ★ Go to the product detail page of this book on **Amazon**
- ★ Scroll down to **Review** this product section
- ★ Click **Write a customer review** in the Customer Reviews section
- ★ Select a Star Rating
- ★ Scribble your happy thoughts, add photos and videos. Submit!

Thank you in advance for your review ♥

Made in the USA
Las Vegas, NV
30 May 2024

90511452R00063